COM
MEXI

A MEXICAN
COOKBOOK

BY ROSA
CIENFUEGOS

IDA CANA

SNACKS, TACOS, TORTAS, TAMALES & DESSERTS

Smith Street Books

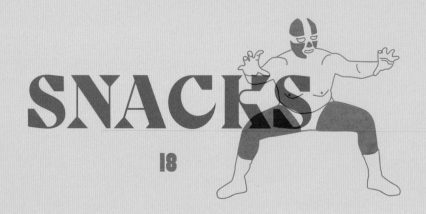

INTRODUCTION

My name is Rosa Cienfuegos. I was born in the heart of 'Chilangolandia' (the affectionate slang term for Mexico City), the largest and most populous city in the Western Hemisphere. I lived in this chaotic, noisy, vibrant and colourful place with its warm people, ancestral traditions and rich culture for 25 years. Although frenetic, I learned to love the city and the craziness that went with it.

When I was young, I travelled throughout Mexico visiting family and friends, and immersing myself in our country's vast history and unique gastronomy. I learned about regional food and centuries-old dishes that are still made using traditional cooking techniques and equipment. I rarely ate the same dish twice as there was always something new to try. Every house I visited had a signature family recipe that would be slightly different from the last. These recipes had been passed down through the generations and were often closely guarded secrets, treasured by their custodians. I came to realise that they were part of each and every family. They had witnessed laughter, tears and heated discussions, but most importantly the happiness that comes from eating together. This influential part of my life gave me an understanding and love for Mexico and its people, our rich culture, traditions and, of course, our food.

I have always loved Mexican food. As a child, I remember visiting the markets near our family home with my mum and my grandma. I loved walking through the laneways full of fresh colourful produce, visiting the food stalls with their enticing smells and the Mexican drinks made fresh to order to cool you down on a hot summer's day.

Food is very important to Mexicans. It reconnects us to our past, our families and our feelings; it touches emotions that are always in our hearts, from the memory of our grandmas pottering in the kitchen to mothers teaching their children how to cook.

It was this love that led me Australia to live with my father 10 years after he left Mexico. The idea of moving to Australia had been in my mind for many years. I was a young single mum living in Mexico City and I missed my father terribly. For Mexicans, family is more important than anything else, so one day I finally made the decision to give away my belongings, jump on a plane and move to the other side of the world.

Dad was living in Sydney, along with my brother, sister and nephew. I immediately loved everything about the city – the lifestyle, diversity, multiculturalism and, of course, the opportunity to be reunited with my family. Everything was exciting but there was one thing missing: my beloved Mexican food. At the time, Sydney was not known for its Mexican cuisine and Mexican ingredients were virtually impossible to find. I started to crave the flavours and dishes of my homeland. I needed a gordita with extra chicharrón and salsa verde, but Dad just laughed at me and said, 'that doesn't exist here, my dear'. We visited

Australian Latin American restaurants, but were always disappointed that the food never matched the description on the menu, so in the end we gave up.

The thought of living in another country without the food I had grown up with and held so dear was a bitter pill to swallow, so I started to cook at home, playing with available ingredients and cooking equipment in a bid to achieve authentic Mexican flavours. Luckily, my dad worked as a chef and he happily shared his knowledge, giving me tips and advice along the way. After months of experimenting and cooking at home for family and friends, my dad decided we should open our own Mexican restaurant, El Cuervo Cantina. I started to help him in the kitchen with simple tasks, but I soon became his sous chef. I introduced a few items on the menu, dishes that I really missed and that I hoped would be successful.

Unfortunately, the times didn't match our enthusiasm and the restaurant closed in 2013 leaving behind a disappointed Mexican community. Sadly this community wasn't enough to keep the restaurant going, but it did open up another door, as locals started asking me to cater their parties and family gatherings. My network began to grow and soon I was invited to open a pop-up food stall once a month at the local market.

Word of mouth soon spread and before long my little pop-up stall, La Casa Latina, had regulars beyond the local Mexican community. People would come every month to work their way through my rotating menu and there was always a long line of hungry customers waiting to grab a seat at my small stall. My dad even invited his mariachi band to play while people queued and ate their lunch. It became such a fun place to work!

To this day, I still don't quite understand how La Casa Latina's popularity spread so fast, but soon I was giving interviews and receiving attention on social media. People were even stopping me in the street and calling me the tamale queen, as this was my signature dish.

La Casa Latina created new opportunities for me, and in 2018 I opened Sydney's first tamaleria. It is here that I make fresh tamales every weekend, along with other authentic Mexican street food. I love watching people eating my tamales and talking about how good they are, and it makes me proud to know I have contributed towards the understanding of what real Mexican food tastes like in Sydney.

Of course, I couldn't have done any of this without my dad, my hero, my friend and the person who is behind me all the time. The recipes I use are from his heritage and hard work, and the passion he has, like me, for Mexican gastronomy. We spend a lot of time together, planning, researching, shopping for the best ingredients, driving long distances to find the right products and experimenting with flavours in order to recreate the most authentic dishes possible.

In this book, I give you the recipes that are dear to my heart, those that my dad gave to me, the ones that I have refined over months and years and then shared with new friends, and the most popular dishes from my tamaleria. These recipes are truly Mexican and full of love. I hope you enjoy them.

With love for all of you and for Mexico, Rosa Cienfuegos.

THE MEXICAN PANTRY

FROM MEXICO TO THE WORLD

Most of the following ingredients are proudly 100 per cent Mexican and you'll find many of them in the recipes in this book. The majority can be purchased from Latin American supermarkets or online.

ACHIOTE

Sold in small blocks, this paste made from annatto seeds is often used to give a radiant colour and sour flavour to food. It is one of the signature ingredients of Yucatan cuisine.

AMARANTH

A 'pseudo-cereal' native to South America. The edible seeds of the amaranth plant are one of the oldest cultivated crops in the world. In Mexico, it is popularly used to make Alegrias (see page 178), an amaranth and agave syrup–pressed candy bar with nuts and sultanas that's commonly eaten as a snack.

AVOCADOS

The avocado was first discovered around 500 BC by the Aztecs who named it āhuacatl, meaning 'testicle', due to the way the fruit hangs on trees. Today, the humble avocado, of which Mexico is still the world's biggest producer, is found in every Mexican home where it's added to everything from tacos to tortas, dips to salsas, or just scooped with a spoon. Even if your meal doesn't call for avocado, we still often serve a cheeky avocado taco at the start or end of the main meal.

BEANS

These dried legumes are a staple in every Mexican household. Generally speaking, pinto beans are more commonly found in Mexico's north, while black beans are used in central and southern Mexican cooking. Beans are used to make Frijoles refritos (see page 53), which is used as a spread or filling for tacos and tortas.

CACAO

Is there anyone who doesn't like chocolate? Perhaps Mexico's most famous export, cacao was worshipped, used as currency and consumed as a bitter drink before the arrival of the Spanish in the 16th century. They took the cacao bean to Europe where sugar was added to make the much-loved treat we all know and love today (although some Mexicans will argue that Mexican chocolate is still the best). Abuelita or Ibarra are two of Mexico's most famous chocolate brands and you will find chocolate in some form or another in every Mexican kitchen. We eat cacao to treat depression, sadness, colds and flu or use it to make mole or any number of sweet treats.

CAJETA

A thickened syrup made with burned goat's milk, cajeta is considered a type of dulce de leche. Eaten as a snack with warm bolillos (Mexican bread rolls) it can also be used to make jellies and cakes or to top ice cream and pancakes.

CHAMOY

This versatile condiment made with fresh or dried apricots, chillies and tangy lime powder adds a delightful tang to dishes and drinks. It is most commonly served with fruit, fries, chicarrones and even in cocktails.

CHEESE

Oaxaca cheese (also known as quesillo) is a white semi-hard cheese from, unsurprisingly, Oaxaca. It is one of Mexico's most popular cheeses and it is used in any dish that requires melted cheese. Fresco cheese (or fresh cheese) is commonly used to top garnachas, soups, enchiladas and tostadas. A mild feta is a good alternative. Asadero cheese is a hard cheese similar to halloumi that's popular in the north of Mexico. Requesón is a soft, sour cheese that's also used to top garnachas or tacos. Ricotta is a good substitute.

CHILLIES

There are over 150 varieties of chilli in Mexico, along with countless ways to prepare them. Some of the most popular include serrano, jalapeno, chipotle, guajillo and chilli de àrbol and you will find these chillies used in many of the recipes in this book in both their fresh and dried form. Dried chillies are easy to buy in bulk online. For more information about chillies in Mexican cuisine check out pages 66–67.

CORN

The foundation of Mexican cuisine, corn is Mexico's most common grain, with 59 indigenous varieties to choose from.

It forms the basis of tamales, tacos, quesadillas, gorditas, tostadas, desserts and drinks. It is estimated that corn is the main ingredient in more than half of all Mexican dishes and tortillas are nearly always served with the main meal. In Mexico, white, yellow and blue corn is most commonly ground into flour for tortillas. Huitlacoche (corn smut) is a corn fungus which grows on some corn and is considered to be a truffle-like delicacy that's added to tacos and other dishes.

CREAM

Thickened cream or sour cream are must-have ingredients for topping garnachas, enchiladas and chilaquiles and for making desserts. I like to add half thickened cream and half sour cream when adding cream to my savoury dishes.

EPAZOTE

This aromatic herb native to Central America is often added to beans, quesadillas, soups and teas. It has a strong, almost medicinal flavour that adds depth to dishes, but it can be an acquired taste to anyone eating it for the first time. Epazote has medicinal properties that can aid digestion and reduce bloating, although consuming too much can lead to an upset stomach.

JICAMA

Also known as the Mexican yam bean, this tuberous root vegetable is added to salads or eaten as a street snack with various toppings (check out the Jicaletas on page 46).

LIMES

Although not indigenous to Mexico, it's impossible to imagine a Mexican meal without the addition of this ubiquitous citrus fruit. Limes are served with tacos, garnachas, seafood, desserts or in cocktails, adding a sour tang, which helps to cut through rich flavours.

MAGGI SAUCE

Added to seafood or sprinkled over snacks and micheladas (Mexican beer cocktails), Maggi sauce adds a salty, umami taste to dishes.

MASA

The resulting dough from mixing nixtamalized corn flour (masa harina) and water, masa is used to make tortillas, quesadillas, gorditas, sopes, huaraches and more. Do not confuse nixtamalized corn flour with regular corn meal or flour when buying flour to make your tortilla dough.

NOPALES

Also known as the prickly pear cactus, nopales are the edible pads of the nopales cactus and are sold fresh and tinned throughout Mexico. They have a mild and slightly sour flavour, as well as being slightly sticky. Sliced and cooked nopales are often added to tacos or served in salads. In Mexico, nopales and the fruit from the cactus are added to juices and smoothies. Outside of Mexico, the tinned variety is readily available.

ONIONS

Like many cuisines, onions feature heavily in Mexican cooking. White onions, which are sweeter and less astringent than regular brown onions, are nearly always used. They are often added raw to salsas and salads or used as a garnish.

TAJIN

A chilli, lime and salt powder with a sour taste that's often sprinkled on fruit, vegetables, beer, popcorn, lollies and even soups. It goes with everything!

TAMAROCA STICKS

Mexican candy sticks made with tamarind, chilli, lime and salt. They are often added to slurpees or micheladas, but can also be enjoyed on their own.

TOMATILLOS

Also known as the Mexican husk tomato, despite their name tomatillos are not related to tomatoes. The fruit has a tangy, sour taste and can be eaten cooked or raw. It is one of the main ingredients in salsa verde.

TOMATOES

A global ingredient synonymous with Mediterranean cuisine, it's hard to imagine Europe has only grown this fruit for 500 years. Archaeological evidence suggests the Aztecs were cultivating and cooking tomatoes as early as 500 BC. By the 16th century, Cortes and his fellow invaders spread this versatile fruit around the world and the rest, as they say, is history.

VALENTINA SAUCE

This famous Mexican condiment is a staple in kitchens throughout Mexico. It combines cayenne chillies, vinegar and salt to produce a hot sauce that's drizzled on nearly everything: fruit, vegetables, pizza, popcorn, soups, beer, chips and even a breakfast quesadilla. Valentina sauce comes in two varieties – hot and extra hot. You can replace it with Buffalo, Tapatio or Botanera hot sauces, but Valentina sauce is the most traditional.

VANILLA

Another indigenous ingredient, vanilla comes from the orchid family and grows in tropical areas. Pollination is required to produce the vanilla 'fruit' with its dark shiny skin and strong perfume. Vanilla seeds are added to many Mexican desserts.

CKS

SNACKS SNACKS SNACKS

Indulging in snacks is an everyday event for Mexicans. From a refreshing fruit salad to start the day to a pan-fried sausage cut in the shape of an octopus, snacks are a quintessential comfort that help ease the daily stresses of life. Every state has its own interpretation of these addictive morsels, and some can only be found in specific regions due to the availability of produce and the culinary preferences of its snack-loving residents.

Located on nearly every street corner and with a huge range of options, Mexican snacks are always cheap and generally loaded with chilli, lime and salt, whether they're savoury or sweet. It's highly recommended to seek out as many stalls as possible as individual food vendors like to let their creativity run wild and, as a result, no two dishes are ever quite the same. This ultimately means a never-ending choice and a lifetime of unique dishes waiting to be discovered on the Mexican doorstep.

ESQUITES Y ELOTES

CORN IN A CUP

Esquites, also known as elote en vaso, are sold by eloteros – street-food vendors with a passion for corn. Slathered in creamy, cheesy goodness and finished with chilli and lime, esquites are enjoyed as a late-afternoon snack throughout Mexico. Thankfully, they are also super easy to make at home.

The stock here is optional, so feel free to use water instead if you prefer.

SERVES 4

UNSALTED BUTTER	10 G (⅓ OZ)
TABLE SALT	10 G (⅓ OZ)
EPAZOTE LEAVES (OPTIONAL)	10 G (⅓ OZ)
DRIED CHILLIES DE ÁRBOL OR GUAJILLO CHILLIES, FINELY CHOPPED	2
WHITE OR YELLOW SWEETCORN KERNELS, STRIPPED FROM THE COB	500 G (1 LB 2 OZ)
CHICKEN STOCK OR WATER, PLUS EXTRA IF NEEDED	1 LITRE (34 FL OZ/4 CUPS)
WHOLE-EGG MAYONNAISE	200 G (7 OZ)
LIMES, JUICED	2
COTIJA OR FRESCO CHEESE, CRUMBLED	40 G (1½ OZ)
CAYENNE PEPPER OR TAJIN	FOR SPRINKLING
LIME WEDGES	TO SERVE

Melt the butter in a large frying pan over medium heat and add the salt, epazote (if using) and chilli. Cook, stirring, for 5 minutes or until the chilli is soft and starting to change colour. Add the corn kernels and continue to cook, stirring frequently, for 10 minutes or until lightly golden.

Add the chicken stock or water, then cover and cook for 15 minutes or until the kernels are soft and cooked through and most of the liquid has been absorbed. If the corn starts to look dry, add a little more stock or water as needed.

Divide half the kernel mixture among four cups, leaving most of the stock behind. Stir through half the mayonnaise, half the lime juice and half the cheese, and sprinkle over a little cayenne pepper or tajin. Add the remaining corn, mayonnaise, lime juice and cheese and finish with a final sprinkling of cayenne or tajin. Enjoy with lime wedges.

SNACKS

GRILLED CORN ON THE COB

Another way Mexicans like to enjoy corn is, naturally, on the cob. Here, the neutral flavour of white sweetcorn provides endless opportunities for flavours and toppings but, of course, you can use yellow corn, too. Let's do it the Mexican way!

Carefully remove the husks and silks from the corn, keeping the husks as complete as possible. Reserve five of the husks and discard the silks.

Skewer the corn with metal skewers or corn forks.

Bring a large saucepan of water to the boil over high heat. Add the corn and salt and gently place the reserved husks on top to cover the corn. Reduce the heat to a simmer and cook the corn for 10 minutes or until soft and cooked through.

Drain the corn for 5 minutes or until they are completely dry. You can also dry them using a clean tea towel to speed up the process. Squeeze the lime halves over the corn.

Spread the mayonnaise on a plate and roll the corn in the mayonnaise. Scatter the cheese all over the corn and generously sprinkle with the chilli, cayenne, paprika or tajin.

MAKES 10

WHITE OR YELLOW SWEETCORN COBS	10
TABLE SALT	30 G (1 OZ)
LIME, HALVED, PLUS LIME WEDGES TO SERVE	1
WHOLE-EGG MAYONNAISE	300 G (10½ OZ)
COTIJA OR FRESCO CHEESE, CRUMBLED	150 G (5½ OZ)
CHILLI POWDER, CAYENNE PEPPER, SWEET PAPRIKA OR TAJIN	FOR SPRINKLING

Slam! Corn! Pow!

ELOTES

TOTOPOS

 **TORTILLA CHIPS**

Outside of Mexico, 'totopos' are known as good ol' tortilla chips. Yes, you can buy them in large bags of myriad flavours from the supermarket, but they are super easy to make at home and taste mucho, mucho better! Once you've got the hang of it, you can create many other Mexican dishes including chilaquiles (see page 147), sopa de tortilla and, of course, nachos.

I remember eating totopos as a starter or welcoming snack at restaurants or cantinas when I was younger. They are usually served with refried beans, pico de gallo, guacamole or cheese dip.

MAKES 500 G (1 LB 2 OZ)

VEGETABLE OIL	500 ML (17 FL OZ/2 CUPS)
FRESHLY MADE CORN TORTILLAS (SEE PAGE 196)	12
TABLE SALT	TO TASTE
SERVING IDEAS	
FRIJOLES NEGROS (SEE PAGE 202)	–
PICO DE GALLO (SEE PAGE 205)	–
SALSA ROJA (SEE PAGE 207)	–
CHEESE DIP (STORE-BOUGHT IS FINE)	–

Heat the oil in a large heavy-based saucepan over medium–high heat to 180°C (350°F) on a kitchen thermometer.

Cut the tortillas into eight rough triangles then, working in batches so as not to overcrowd the pan, add the tortilla triangles to the hot oil and fry them for 3 minutes, turning them over until crisp and lightly golden.

Remove the tortillas using a slotted spoon and transfer to a large plate lined with paper towel to drain. Season with salt, to taste.

Serve the totopos with your favourite accompaniments or use them to make the chilaquiles on page 147 or nachos.

CHARRITOS

CORN FRIES

Charritos or 'churritos' are delicious deep-fried corn strips that Mexicans usually cover with hot sauce and fresh lime. They are the perfect snack to share with friends and family while out and about, perhaps strolling through the park or walking home from school. I often make them when hosting Mexican parties, and I love seeing all my friends devouring them and then asking for the recipe. Give them a go!

SERVES 4-6

VEGETABLE OIL	500 ML (17 FL OZ/2 CUPS)
MASA FLOUR	1 KG (2 LB 3 OZ)
BAKING POWDER	1 TABLESPOON
TABLE SALT	30 G (1 OZ)
FRESHLY GROUND BLACK PEPPER	1 TEASPOON
LARD	2 TABLESPOONS
WARM WATER	875 ML (29½ FL OZ)
LIMES, HALVED	2
VALENTINA, BOTANERA, TAPATIO, CHOLULA OR BUFFALO HOT SAUCE	TO SERVE

Heat the oil in a large heavy-based saucepan over medium–high heat to 180°C (350°F) on a kitchen thermometer.

Combine the masa flour, baking powder, salt, pepper and lard in a large bowl. Slowly add the warm water and mix until you have a soft and pliable dough.

Working in batches, place the dough in a piping bag with a 5 mm (¼ in) nozzle attached. Pipe out 5 cm (2 in) length charritos and place on a tray lined with baking paper.

Working in batches, fry the charritos, turning occasionally, for 2 minutes or until golden and cooked through. Transfer to a plate lined with paper towel to drain.

Leave the charritos to cool for at least 1 hour, then transfer to a serving bowl. Squeeze in the lime juice and toss through. Serve with plenty of hot sauce drizzled over the top or on the side for dipping.

SALCHIPULPOS

OCTOPUS SAUSAGES

The name 'salchipulpos' is a combination of the Mexican words for sausage, 'salchicha' and octopus, 'pulpos'. Each sausage is sliced to make it look like an octopus and then either baked or shallow-fried and served with fries, lime juice and Valentina hot sauce. As well as being a popular street snack, 'salchipulpos' are perfect for parties – get creative and serve them with your favourite salsa, salad, mash or melted cheese.

SERVES 4

FRANKFURT OR COCKTAIL SAUSAGES, SUCH AS PORK, TURKEY OR CHICKEN	500 G (1 LB 2 OZ)
VEGETABLE OIL	125 ML (4 FL OZ/½ CUP)
TO SERVE	
TOMATO KETCHUP	–
AMERICAN MUSTARD (OPTIONAL)	–
VALENTINA HOT SAUCE	–
LIME WEDGES	–
MAGGI SAUCE (OPTIONAL)	–
FRIES	–

Cut the sausages in half and make eight incisions from the cut end into the middle of each sausage half. These will be the octopus tentacles.

Heat the oil in a large saucepan over medium heat. Working in batches, add the sausages and shallow-fry, turning occasionally, for 3 minutes or until golden and crisp on all sides.

Using a slotted spoon, remove the salchipulpos and transfer to a plate lined with paper towel to drain. Place the salchipulpos on a serving platter and serve warm drizzled with tomato ketchup, mustard (if using), Valentina hot sauce, lime juice, a few drops of Maggi sauce (if using) and, of course, a big bowl of fries.

TLAYUDAS

MEXICAN PIZZAS

I remember eating tlayudas every time I went to el Zócalo – Mexico City's central plaza – where the local ladies sold them directly from their baskets on pieces of butcher's paper.

Tlayudas originally come from Oaxaca where they are traditionally topped with meat and the local Oaxacan cheese, quesillo. This recipe, however, is more commonly found in Mexico City where tlayudas are simpler and eaten as a snack rather than a main meal. Feel free to add extra toppings, such as fried chorizo, cured meat or even fried grasshoppers for a truly authentic experience!

MAKES 10

CHOPPED WHITE ONION	100 G (3½ OZ)
CHOPPED CORIANDER (CILANTRO) LEAVES	100 G (3½ OZ)
VEGETABLE OIL SPRAY	-
FRIJOLES REFRITOS (SEE PAGE 53)	250 G (9 OZ)
FRESH OR TINNED NOPALES, ROUGHLY CHOPPED	500 G (1 LB 2 OZ)
FRESCO CHEESE OR FETA, GRATED	100 G (3½ OZ)
SALSA VERDE (SEE PAGE 206)	TO SERVE

TLAYUDAS

BLUE MASA FLOUR	500 G (1 LB 2 OZ)
WARM WATER	600 ML (20½ FL OZ)
TABLE SALT	PINCH

To make the tlayudas, mix all the ingredients by hand in a bowl until the dough is soft and not sticky.

Place the onion and coriander in a bowl and mix to combine. Set aside.

Heat a comal or heavy-based frying pan over high heat and spray with oil.

Place a square of plastic wrap over the bottom half of a tortilla press. Roll 100 g (3½ oz) of the dough into a ball and place it in the middle of the tortilla press. Cover with another square of plastic wrap (this ensures the dough doesn't stick to the press). Close the tortilla press and gently press to flatten the dough into a disc at least 3 mm (⅛ in) thick.

Open the tortilla press, remove the top layer of plastic wrap and flip the tortilla onto your hand. Remove the bottom layer of plastic wrap and place the tlayuda in the pan. Cook for about 3 minutes each side until hard and crisp. Remove from the pan and repeat with the remaining dough to make 10 tlayudas.

Evenly spread the frijoles refritos over the base of each tlayuda. Top with the nopales, onion and coriander and grated cheese. Finish with a good dollop of salsa verde and dig in!

NOTE
Don't pre-make the tlayudas dough as it will dry out, making it harder to handle.

ALITAS DE POLLO

CHICKEN WINGS

These chicken wings are a popular night-time snack often sold outside metro stations in Mexico City, where their smokey aroma lures people in on their way home after a night out. They also make an excellent snack to eat with a cold beer while watching the local soccer game on a Sunday afternoon. I strongly suggest you make a double batch!

MAKES 20

VEGETABLE OIL	500 ML (17 FL OZ/2 CUPS)
CHICKEN WINGS, HALVED	10
UNSALTED BUTTER	40 G (1½ OZ)
VALENTINA, BOTANERA, TAPATIO, CHOLULA OR BUFFALO HOT SAUCE	150 ML (5 FL OZ)
TOMATO KETCHUP	150 ML (5 FL OZ)
GARLIC POWDER	PINCH
WHITE VINEGAR	1 TABLESPOON
WORCESTERSHIRE SAUCE	1 TABLESPOON
TABLE SALT	PINCH
LIMES, HALVED	3

Heat the oil in a very large heavy-based saucepan over medium–high heat to 160°C (320°F) on a kitchen thermometer.

Add the wings to the hot oil and cook, turning occasionally, for 5 minutes, then reduce the heat to 130°C (265°F) and continue to cook for 20 minutes or until they are dark golden and very crisp.

Using a slotted spoon, remove the wings and transfer to a tray lined with paper towel to drain.

Melt the butter in a large frying pan over medium-low heat, add the hot sauce, tomato ketchup, garlic powder, white vinegar and Worcestershire sauce and stir for 2–3 minutes, until the sauce turns dark red.

Add the wings to the pan and stir to coat in the sauce. Season with a tiny pinch of salt, then remove from the heat and transfer to a large serving plate. Squeeze over the lime juice and serve with cold beer!

SNACKS

STREET-FOOD STALLS

There is no better way to experience Mexico's food diversity than to wander through the streets of any city, stopping at local street-food vendors to sample their wares. The large number of street-food stalls in Mexico creates a competitive atmosphere, which brings out well-practised marketing skills that vary from silly menus and fun descriptions of dishes to brightly decorated stalls and an amazing array of condiments.

Each stall has a different set-up according to what they are selling, as the utensils and cooking equipment required depend on what's being sold: a tamales stall only needs a steamer with a heating element and a small table for serving, whereas a carnitas stall is a bigger affair with a huge copper pot, a distinctive burner and a large wooden shovel. Canasta tacos are often transported in a wicker basket at the back of a bicycle, while garnachas generally need more space for deep-frying, a table for all the toppings and space for two people serving. Many other street-style tacos and tortas are served out of a more solid stall that might have a permanent spot on the street, but often without seats or tables. If you are craving something sweet, it's easy to find vendors walking in and around permanent markets with a basket containing their specialised desserts.

For most Mexicans, street-food stalls offer more than just a meal on the go. It is a way of life that brings loved ones, family and friends together to enjoy their favourite dishes at affordable prices.

SNACKS

CHICHARRONES PREPARADOS

PREPARED
CHICHARRONES

Chicharrones are adored by all Mexicans, so much so that you can find them for sale on nearly every street corner throughout the country. You probably know chicharrones as deep-fried crispy pork skin, but chicharrones can also be made from wheat flour and either served as crispy wheel-shaped bite-sized snacks or, as I have done here, in thin rectangular sheets that are deep-fried and served with any number of toppings.

MAKES 16

PLAIN (ALL-PURPOSE) FLOUR	200 G (7 OZ)
TABLE SALT	2 TABLESPOONS
BAKING POWDER	40 G (1½ OZ)
VEGETABLE OIL, PLUS EXTRA FOR GREASING	1 LITRE (34 FL OZ/4 CUPS)
CUERITOS	
PORK SKIN, CUT INTO 1 CM x 5 CM (½ x 2 IN) LONG STRIPS	300 G (10½ OZ)
TABLE SALT	60 G (2 OZ)
BLACK PEPPERCORNS	3
LIME, JUICED	1
WHITE ONION, PEELED	½
GARLIC CLOVE	1
DRIED BAY LEAVES	3
WHITE VINEGAR	2 TEASPOONS
TO ASSEMBLE	
THICKENED CREAM	300 ML (10½ FL OZ)
SMALL ICEBERG LETTUCE OR CABBAGE, FINELY SHREDDED	1
TOMATOES, THINLY SLICED	3
AVOCADOS, THINLY SLICED	3
LIMES, HALVED	8
TABLE SALT	PINCH PER SLAB
FRESCO CHEESE, CRUMBLED	150 G (5½ OZ)
VALENTINA, BOTANERA, TAPATIO, CHOLULA OR BUFFALO HOT SAUCE	TO SERVE

Sift the flour into a large bowl and stir through the salt and baking powder. Add 750 ml (25½ fl oz/3 cups) water and stir until there are no visible lumps. Pour the mixture into a large non-stick saucepan and place over medium heat. Stir the mixture for 10–15 minutes, until it becomes a solid non-sticky flour paste that comes away easily from the side of the pan.

Grease two baking trays with oil, then spread the warm flour paste over the two trays in even layers, about ½ cm (¼ in) thick. Cover with a tea towel and set outside in the sun to dehydrate. This might take up to 10 hours depending on the weather. During this time, the flour paste will turn brown with a solid but flexible consistency.

Meanwhile, to make the cueritos, place the pork skin, half the salt, the peppercorns and lime juice in a large saucepan. Cover with water and bring to the boil. Boil for 15 minutes, then drain and rinse the pork skin under cold running water. Return the pork skin to the pan and add the onion, garlic, bay leaves, vinegar and remaining salt. Cover with water, bring to the boil again over high heat and cook for 5 minutes – the skin should be soft but not soggy. Drain again, then transfer the pork skin to a bowl and set aside in the fridge. Discard the remaining ingredients.

Using a sharp knife, cut each wheat slab into eight 10 cm × 15 cm (4 in × 6 in) rectangles to make 16 pieces.

Heat the oil in a large saucepan over medium–high heat to 180°C (350°F) on a kitchen thermometer. Working in batches, add the wheat slabs and deep-fry for 2 minutes, turning occasionally, until puffed up and lightly golden. Remove using a slotted spoon and drain on paper towel.

To assemble the chicharrones, spread each slab with thickened cream and top with the lettuce or cabbage, tomato and avocado. Squeeze over the lime halves and add the cueritos and salt. Finish with more cream, the cheese and a drizzle of hot sauce.

ESCAMOCHAS

FRUIT SALAD

A healthy (or perhaps not!) snack to start your day, an escamocha is a fruit salad served with your choice of honey and muesli or whipped cream and chocolate sprinkles. I've added all of these ingredients to this recipe as it's how I like to eat it, but you can, of course, pick and mix to suit your tastes. Escamochas are sold at markets early in the morning where punters eat them for breakfast, but I also remember eating them after school. They were extremely refreshing under the hot Mexican sun!

SERVES 8

WATERMELON, CUT INTO CHUNKS	150 G (5½ OZ)
ROCKMELON (CANTALOUPE), CUT INTO CHUNKS	150 G (5½ OZ)
GOLDEN DELICIOUS APPLE, CORED AND CUT INTO CHUNKS	150 G (5½ OZ)
PAPAYA, CUT INTO CHUNKS	150 G (5½ OZ)
PINEAPPLE, CUT INTO CHUNKS	150 G (5½ OZ)
STRAWBERRIES, HALVED	4
SHREDDED COCONUT	30 G (1 OZ / ½ CUP)
MUESLI	100 G (3½ OZ)
ORANGE JUICE	80 ML (2¾ FL OZ / ⅓ CUP)
HONEY	3 TABLESPOONS
WHIPPED CREAM, PLUS EXTRA TO SERVE	80 G (2½ OZ)
CHOCOLATE SPRINKLES	TO SERVE

Place all the fruit apart from the strawberries in a large bowl and mix to combine. Add 1 tablespoon of mixed fruit to eight tumblers then sprinkle over a little coconut and muesli. Drizzle over a small amount of orange juice and honey and add 2 teaspoons of whipped cream. Repeat this layering until all the ingredients have been used.

Finish with a final spoonful of whipped cream and perch a strawberry half on top. Scatter over a few chocolate sprinkles and serve immediately.

MANGONADAS

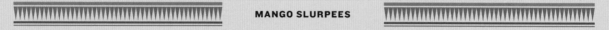

MANGO SLURPEES

It doesn't need to be summer to find a range of raspados (slurpees) sold throughout Mexico City's streets, and in the world of iced drinks the mangonada is definitely my favourite. The marriage of sweet mango and sour lime is a uniquely refreshing experience, especially on a hot day in the craziness of the city or while relaxing on the beach. Try to seek out chamoy if you can; it adds a delightful finishing tang to drinks and fruit dishes.

SERVES 4

MANGOES, ROUGHLY CHOPPED	2
FROZEN MANGO CHUNKS	500 G (1 LB 2 OZ)
LIME SORBET	130 G (4½ OZ/1 CUP)
LIME, CUT INTO SMALL PIECES	½
ICE CUBES	250 G (9 OZ)
CHAMOY	200 ML (7 OZ)
TAJIN	TO SPRINKLE
TAMAROCA STICKS (OPTIONAL)	4

Place the fresh and frozen mango, lime sorbet, lime pieces and ice in a blender and blend until well combined.

Place 2 tablespoons of chamoy in the base of four glasses. Divide half the blended mango mixture among the glasses and top with three shakes of tajin and another 2 teaspoons of chamoy. Add the remaining mango mixture and finish with a little extra tajin and a tamaroca stick (if using).

Enjoy immediately!

SNACKS

JICALETAS

JICAMAS ON STICKS

If you are visiting Mexico City, please seek out a jicaleta stall! Jicaletas are slices of jicama that have been soaked in chamoy, sprinkled with miguelito – a Mexican candy chilli powder – and served on a popsicle stick. They may look like a kids' snack, but I promise you they are equally enjoyed by adults. I remember taking my son to the park in the centre of Azcapotzalco, a municipality in Mexico City, and buying him a rainbow jicaleta. I ended up with a child smothered in rainbow sugar on his cheeks, hands and lips!

As miguelito powder can be hard to find outside of Mexico, I've provided an easy recipe to make at home that's as good as the real thing.

MAKES 24

LARGE JICAMAS (YAM BEANS), PEELED AND SLICED LENGTHWAYS INTO 2.5 CM (1 IN) THICK SLICES	3
FRESHLY SQUEEZED LIME JUICE	250 ML (8½ FL OZ/1 CUP)
CHAMOY	250 ML (8½ FL OZ/1 CUP)
MIGUELITO POWDER	
CASTER (SUPERFINE) SUGAR	100 G (3½ OZ)
CHILLI POWDER	30 G (1 OZ)
YOUR CHOICE OF VEGETABLE COLOURING POWDER (OPTIONAL)	1 TEASPOON

To make the miguelito powder, combine all the ingredients in a small bowl, then tip onto a flat plate.

Insert a wooden popsicle stick into the base of each jicama slice, so it resembles a popsicle.

Place the lime juice and chamoy in separate shallow bowls. Working with one jicama slice at a time, dip both sides in the lime juice, followed by the chamoy, then press into the miguelito powder.

Hand the jicaleta to the first lucky recipient, then continue with the remaining ingredients.

SNACKS

ACHAS

GARNACHAS
GARNACHAS
GARNACHAS
GARNACHAS
GARNACHAS

Better known as 'antojitos Mexicanos', meaning 'Mexican little bites', garnachas are sold on Mexico's streets from early morning until the day is done. Vendors position their stalls at bus stops and metro stations during the day, but come the early evening, they take their carts home and set up in their backyards or outside their homes and invite the neighbourhood round to hang out and enjoy a simple 'fast-food' supper.

Mexicans always have their favourite garnachas stall and vendors will often remember individuals' favourite combinations and toppings. It's like your mum is cooking delicious greasy food right in front of you – she knows what you like and the way you like it!

Every region of Mexico has its own interpretation of antojitos, from simple fillings of salsa and onion to more elaborate dishes including shredded chicken, chorizo, huitlacoche or pulled pork.

Masa forms the base of almost all garnachas with often the only differences being the size, shape and thickness of the dough.

When I moved to Sydney, I started my own garnachas stall with the help of my friend Elenita, to recreate the dishes I missed most. It made me understand the intense labour required and the love that goes into every dish as you make everything from scratch. This chapter will definitely bring you closer to some of Mexico's most authentic dishes.

SOPES DE FRIJOLES NEGROS

SOPES WITH BLACK BEANS

Sopes are a classic Mexican garnacha that can be found at many street-food stalls. They are most popular in central and southern Mexico, and each region has its own interpretation. Sopes are small but thick tortillas with pinched edges that are topped with beans, lettuce and salsa, vegetables, such as potato or cabbage, or even just salsa and cheese.

MAKES 10

FRESHLY COOKED SOPES (SEE PAGE 197)	10
FRIJOLES REFRITOS	
VEGETABLE OIL	2 TABLESPOONS
WHITE ONION, DICED	½
TOMATOES, DICED	3
FRIJOLES NEGROS (SEE PAGE 202)	250 G (9 OZ)
COOKING LIQUID FROM THE FRIJOLES NEGROS, PLUS EXTRA IF NEEDED	150 ML (5½ FL OZ)
EPAZOTE (OPTIONAL)	PINCH
TO SERVE	
ICEBERG LETTUCE, SHREDDED	1
THICKENED CREAM OR SOUR CREAM (I LIKE TO USE HALF AND HALF)	250 ML (8½ FL OZ/1 CUP)
FRESCO CHEESE, COTIJA OR FETA, CRUMBLED	250 G (9 OZ)
SALSA DE CHIPOTLE (SEE PAGE 213)	TO SERVE

To make the frijoles refritos, heat the oil in a saucepan over medium heat. Add the onion and tomato and cook for 4 minutes or until softened.

Add the frijoles negros and the cooking liquid and stir through. Using a potato masher, crush the beans until they are half mashed, adding a little extra cooking liquid if the mixture is very thick.

Add the epazote (if using) and stir the beans for 3 minutes. Remove from the heat.

Spread a thick layer of frijoles refritos over each sope. Top with the lettuce, cream and cheese and spoon over a healthy amount of salsa de chipotle.

PAPADILLAS

████████████████████ **POTATO QUESADILLAS** ████████████████████

Papadillas can be found throughout Mexico, although the name may vary from state to state. Deep-fried and topped with lettuce and salsa, papadillas are a delicious vegetarian garnacha that will leave you licking your fingers after every bite.

MAKES 10

SMALL ALL-PURPOSE POTATOES	200 G (7 OZ)
TABLE SALT	2 TEASPOONS
VEGETABLE OIL	FOR COOKING
WHITE ONION, DICED	½
LARGE GARLIC CLOVE, MINCED	1
FRESH JALAPENO, SERRANO OR CAYENNE CHILLIES, CHOPPED	5
FRESHLY MADE 11 CM (4¼ IN) CORN TORTILLAS (SEE PAGE 196), WARMED	10

TO SERVE

SHREDDED ICEBERG LETTUCE	–
SALSA VERDE (SEE PAGE 206)	–
GUACAMOLE (SEE PAGE 204)	–
COTIJA OR FRESCO CHEESE, CRUMBLED	–
CORIANDER (CILANTRO) LEAVES	–

Place the whole potatoes in a saucepan and cover with cold water. Bring to the boil over medium–high heat, then reduce the heat and simmer for 10 minutes or until the potatoes are cooked through.

Drain the potatoes and transfer to a large bowl, then mash them with the salt. You can peel them if you like, but I don't bother.

Heat 1 tablespoon of vegetable oil in a large frying pan over medium–high heat. Add the onion, garlic and chilli and cook, stirring frequently, for 5 minutes or until softened.

Add the onion mixture to the mashed potato and gently combine.

Make a papadilla by adding 50 g (1¾ oz) of the potato mixture to the base of a warm tortilla and folding it in half. Use a tooth pick to secure the quesadilla if it keeps opening up.

Heat 1 cm (½ in) of oil in a frying pan over medium–high heat and add the papadilla. Cook for 1–2 minutes or until the base is crisp, then gently flip and cook the other side until crisp.

Drain the papadilla on a plate lined with paper towel and repeat with the remaining ingredients to make 10 papadillas.

Serve the papadillas with shredded lettuce, salsa verde, guacamole, crumbled cheese and a few coriander leaves and don't forget to remove the tooth picks!

QUESADILLAS FRITAS

Fresh, greasy and filled with Oaxaca cheese or your favourite filling, quesadillas fritas are off-the-scale delicious, yet are surprisingly easy to make. I love eating these delicious morsels as much as I love making them. It reminds me of being back in kindergarten getting my hands messy with playdough.

I recommend using white or yellow masa flour as the hot oil brings out the rich flavour of the masa, giving you a heavenly aftertaste with every quesadilla.

MAKES 10

VEGETABLE OIL	FOR DEEP-FRYING
FRESHLY MADE 11 CM (4¼ IN) CORN TORTILLAS (SEE PAGE 196)	10
OAXACA CHEESE OR FIRM MOZZARELLA, GRATED	500 G (1 LB 2 OZ)
TO SERVE	
SHREDDED ICEBERG LETTUCE	–
COTIJA OR FRESCO CHEESE, CRUMBLED	–
SALSA VERDE (SEE PAGE 206)	–
CORIANDER (CILANTRO) LEAVES	–
LIME WEDGES	–

Heat enough vegetable oil for deep-frying in a large heavy-based saucepan or deep-fryer to 180°C (350°F) on a kitchen thermometer.

Working with one tortilla at a time, scatter 50 g (1¾ oz) of the cheese over the tortilla, then fold the tortilla in half to seal.

Carefully lower the quesadilla into the hot oil and cook, flipping frequently, for 2 minutes or until light golden. Repeat with the remaining tortillas and cheese to make 10 quesadillas.

Top the quesadillas with shredded lettuce, a sprinkling of crumbled cheese, a spoon of salsa verde and a few coriander leaves. Serve with lime wedges.

QUESADILLAS FRITAS

QUESADILLAS DE FLOR DE CALABAZA

 ZUCCHINI FLOWER QUESADILLAS

Do I even need to write a recipe for quesadillas? In Mexico the answer would be no, but outside of the country less is known about the amazing array of ingredients we use to fill these crispy tortillas.

There are two types of quesadilla sold throughout Mexico City: large folded tortillas that are cooked on a griddle, and deep-fried tortillas, which are smaller and topped with lettuce, salsa and cheese (see page 55). Quesadillas might be stuffed with shredded chicken, picadillo (a type of beef and potato stew), pork chicharrones, cheese chicharrones, huitlacoche and cheese, or just cheese. For this recipe, I've focused on the large folded tortillas and filled them with delicate zucchini flowers and Oaxaca cheese.

MAKES 10

VEGETABLE OIL	3 TABLESPOONS
WHITE ONION, DICED	½
FRESH OR TINNED ZUCCHINI (COURGETTE) FLOWERS	100 G (3½ OZ)
TABLE SALT	1 TEASPOON
TORTILLA DOUGH (SEE PAGE 196)	¾ x QUANTITY
OAXACA CHEESE OR FIRM MOZZARELLA, GRATED	500 G (1 LB 2 OZ)
SALSA ROJA (SEE PAGE 207)	TO SERVE

Heat the oil in a frying pan over medium heat, add the onion and sauté for 3 minutes. Add the zucchini flowers and salt and gently stir.

Divide the dough into ten 70 g (2½ oz) dough balls.

Place a square of plastic wrap over the bottom half of an oval tortilla press and place a ball of dough in the middle. Cover with another square of plastic wrap (this ensures the dough doesn't stick to the tortilla press), then close the tortilla press and gently press to flatten the dough into a 26 cm × 11 cm (10¼ in × 4¼ in) oval. Open the tortilla press and remove the top layer of plastic wrap.

Heat a comal or heavy-based frying pan over medium–high heat.

Place 50 g (1¾ oz) of the cheese and 10 g (⅓ oz) of the zucchini flower mixture on the bottom half of the tortilla, then fold the tortilla in half lengthways. Flip the tortilla onto your hand, remove the bottom layer of plastic wrap and place in the pan. Cook, flipping frequently, until the cheese is melted and the quesadilla is slightly crisp. Repeat with the remaining ingredients to make 10 quesadillas.

Serve with salsa roja and enjoy!

NOTE
If you don't have an oval tortilla press, don't worry! Just use a regular tortilla press and roll 50 g (1¾ oz) balls of dough instead. Reduce the amount of filling accordingly.

TOSTADAS DE TINGA DE POLLO

CHICKEN TINGA TOSTADAS

Tostadas are deep-fried tortillas usually topped with a range of cold ingredients. They are crunchy, delicate and can be very messy to eat! But they are also delicious and you can rarely stop at one. The toppings suggested here are just a guide, so feel free to let your imagination run wild.

MAKES 10

VEGETABLE OIL	FOR SHALLOW-FRYING
FRESHLY MADE CORN TORTILLAS (SEE PAGE 196)	10
CHICKEN TINGA	
VEGETABLE OIL	80 ML (2¾ FL OZ/⅓ CUP)
WHITE ONIONS, THINLY SLICED	1½
SALSA DE CHIPOTLE (SEE PAGE 213)	600 ML (20½ FL OZ)
COOKED SHREDDED CHICKEN BREAST	500 G (1 LB 2 OZ)
TABLE SALT	2 TEASPOONS
TOPPINGS	
FRIJOLES REFRITOS (SEE PAGE 53)	250 G (9 OZ)
LARGE ICEBERG LETTUCE, SHREDDED	1
THICKENED OR SOUR CREAM (I LIKE TO USE HALF AND HALF)	250 G (9 OZ/1 CUP)
FRESCO CHEESE, COTIJA OR FETA, CRUMBLED OR GRATED	250 G (9 OZ)
SALSA VERDE (SEE PAGE 206)	200 ML (7 FL OZ)

Heat 100 ml (3½ fl oz) of vegetable oil in a large frying pan over medium heat to 170°C (340°F) on a kitchen thermometer. Working in batches, fry the tortillas, flipping frequently and adding 50 ml (1¾ fl oz) of extra oil to the pan after every three tostadas, for 2 minutes on each side or until they are crisp and lightly golden. If bubbles start to rise in the tortillas when they are cooking, use tongs to pinch the holes together. Transfer the tostadas to a plate lined with paper towel to drain. (If you prefer, you can dry-fry the tortillas in a comal or heavy-based frying pan over low heat, flipping frequently until crisp and ensuring that they don't burn.)

To make the chicken tinga, heat the oil in a large saucepan over medium–high heat, add the onion and cook, stirring frequently, for 5 minutes. Add the salsa de chipotle and stir for 3 minutes or until the salsa turns a dark orange colour. Add the shredded chicken and salt and cook for 5 minutes or until heated through.

Transfer the mixture to a bowl, cover and set aside in the fridge until cool.

Working very gently as the tostadas are fragile and can easily break, spread a thick layer of frijoles refritos on top of each tostada. Top with the chicken tinga, shredded lettuce, cream and cheese. Finish with a spoon of salsa verde and serve.

TOSTADAS DE CARNE EN CHILE PASILLA

PASILLA BEEF TOSTADAS

Beef tostadas are a hit whenever I make them – the rich flavour of pasilla chilli in this dish is unique and definitely a must-try. Beef and chicken tostadas remind me of Mexican Independence celebrations, as this is when they are traditionally sold at pop-up festivals across Mexico City.

MAKES 10

VEGETABLE OIL	FOR SHALLOW-FRYING
FRESHLY MADE CORN TORTILLAS (SEE PAGE 196)	10
PASILLA BEEF	
DRIED PASILLA CHILILES	6
TOMATOES, ROUGHLY CHOPPED	4
TABLE SALT	2 TEASPOONS
VEGETABLE OIL	80 ML (2¾ FL OZ/⅓ CUP)
WHITE ONIONS, THINLY SLICED	1½
WARM WATER	300 ML (10½ FL OZ)
COOKED SHREDDED BEEF	500 G (1 LB 2 OZ)
TOPPINGS	
SOUR CREAM	250 G (9 OZ)
SMALL WHITE CABBAGE, SHREDDED	½
THICKENED CREAM	100 G (3½ OZ)
QUESO FRESCO, COTIJA OR FETA , CRUMBLED OR GRATED	250 G (9 OZ)
SALSA ROJA (SEE PAGE 207)	200 ML (7 FL OZ)

Heat 100 ml (3½ fl oz) of vegetable oil in a large frying pan over medium heat to 170°C (340°F) on a kitchen thermometer. Working in batches, fry the tortillas, flipping frequently and adding 50 ml (1¾ fl oz) of extra oil to the pan after every three tostadas, for 2 minutes on each side or until they are crisp and lightly golden. If bubbles start to rise in the tortillas when they are cooking, use tongs to pinch the holes together. Transfer the tostadas to a plate lined with paper towel to drain. (If you prefer, you can dry-fry the tortillas in a comal or heavy-based frying pan over low heat, flipping frequently until crisp and ensuring that they don't burn.)

To make the pasilla beef, place the chillies in a saucepan and cover with water. Bring to the boil over medium–high heat, then reduce the heat to a simmer and cook for 5 minutes. Drain the chillies and set aside to cool.

Place the chillies, tomato and salt in a blender and pulse to make a thick salsa.

Heat the oil in a large saucepan over medium–high heat, add the onion and sauté for 5 minutes. Add the pasilla chilli mixture and cook, stirring frequently, for 3 minutes, then add the water and stir well to combine. Add the shredded beef and continue to cook, stirring frequently, for 5 minutes or until the beef is heated through.

Transfer the mixture to a bowl, cover and set aside in the fridge until cool.

Working very gently as the tostadas are fragile and can easily break, spread a thick layer of sour cream on top of each tostada. Top with the pasilla beef, a handful of shredded cabbage, a drizzle of thickened cream and a good sprinkling of cheese. Finish with a dollop of salsa roja and serve.

GARNACHAS

TOSTADAS DE CARNE EN CHILE PASILLA

TOSTADAS DE TINGA DE POLLO

CHILLIES

The word chilli (meaning hot pepper) originates from the Nahuatl (Aztec) language, and the chilli plant was one of the first cultivated crops in Mexico (even before corn and tomatoes), where it was widely used for make-up, medicine and rituals, as well as, of course, a signature ingredient in Mexican cooking. Today, chillies are grown extensively throughout the world and it is hard to imagine many cuisines without this ubiquitous ingredient, but in terms of volume, Mexico is still the biggest producer of chillies with over 150 varieties to choose from.

Mexicans cook with the chillies that are available to them locally. Some chillies only grow in specific regions and can rarely be reproduced due to an area's unique soil and weather conditions. Drying chillies is an important process that not only helps us to preserve them for longer, it also brings different flavour profiles and textures to dishes, especially when combined with their fresh counterparts.

Different chillies play different roles in Mexican cuisine and not all of them are used to add heat to a dish. Some provide fruitiness and perfume, while others are fleshy and can be stuffed with multiple ingredients. Fresh and dried chillies form the base of many condiments and they can also be pickled or used as thickeners or colouring agents.

If you don't want your food to be spicy, make sure you remove all the seeds and veins from your chillies, then place the flesh in a container with cold water and a pinch of salt for 5 minutes. Drain and rinse, then proceed with the recipe.

For more information on the chillies used in this book, check out the Mexican pantry on pages 13–15.

PAMBAZOS CON PAPAS Y CHORIZO

POTATO AND CHORIZO PAMBAZOS

It's hard for me to describe a pambazo without gushing as it's my favourite garnacha of all time! There is something so special about the crusty bolillos (bread rolls) soaked in guajillo sauce and filled with chorizo. I used to eat pambazos at least once a week while hanging out with friends in Mexico City. It was the first garnacha I learned to make and I'll never forget burning my fingertips trying to flip it over and watching the sizzling lard splattering over my hands in red guajillo dots. You might need a couple of napkins as this dish is super messy!

MAKES 4

VEGETABLE OIL	3 TABLESPOONS
WHITE ONION, DICED	½
LARGE POTATOES, PEELED AND CUT INTO 3 CM (1¼ IN) DICE, BOILED AND DRAINED	3
TABLE SALT	1 TEASPOON
MEXICAN-STYLE CURED CHORIZO, CHOPPED	200 G (7 OZ)
PORK LARD	1 TABLESPOON
BOLILLOS OR CRUSTY ROLLS, HALVED LENGTHWAYS	4
SMALL ICEBERG LETTUCE, SHREDDED	1
THICKENED CREAM OR SOUR CREAM	250 G (9 OZ)
FRESCO CHEESE, COTIJA OR FETA, CRUMBLED	200 G (7 OZ)
SALSA ROJA (SEE PAGE 207)	TO SERVE
GUAJILLO SAUCE	
DRIED GUAJILLO CHILLIES	8
WHITE ONION, ROUGHLY CHOPPED	½
GARLIC CLOVE	1
TABLE SALT	20 G (¾ OZ)
FRESHLY GROUND BLACK PEPPER	PINCH

To make the guajillo sauce, place the chillies in a saucepan and just cover with water. Bring to the boil over medium–high heat, then reduce the heat to a simmer and cook for 5 minutes. Remove from the heat and set the chillies aside to cool in the water.

Place the chillies and their cooking water, the onion, garlic, salt and pepper in a blender and blend to a runny sauce. Taste and add more salt if necessary. Spread the guajillo sauce on a plate.

Heat the oil in a large frying pan over medium–high heat. Add the onion and cook, stirring frequently, for 7–8 minutes until dark golden. Stir through the potato and salt, then reduce the heat to medium, add the chorizo and cook, stirring, for 10 minutes or until the chorizo is heated through. Set aside.

To assemble the pambazos, heat 1 teaspoon of the lard in a large frying pan over medium–low heat. Working with one bread roll at a time, place the roll, cut side down, in the guajillo sauce, then transfer to the pan and toast for 2 minutes, moving the bread around so it soaks up the lard. Flip the roll over and fill it with a quarter of the potato and chorizo mixture. Close the roll and continue to cook both sides in the pan for 5 minutes or until crisp and golden. Repeat with the remaining ingredients to make four pambazos.

Transfer the pambazos to serving plates, open them up and add a handful of lettuce. Drizzle over the cream, sprinkle with the cheese and finish with salsa roja. Put the tops back on and dive in.

GORDITAS DE CHICHARRÓN

CHICARRÓN GORDITAS

Deep-fried, pan-fried or just plain grilled, I guarantee you will fall in love with gorditas. They might look simple and perhaps not the best-looking garnacha, but the chicharrón prensado used to fill these gorditas has a unique and unforgettable flavour. I serve them daily at my tamaleria in Sydney and I always sell out!

MAKES 6

VEGETABLE OIL	FOR DEEP-FRYING
TORTILLA DOUGH (SEE PAGE 196)	¾ x QUANTITY
WHITE ONION, FINELY CHOPPED	70 G (2½ OZ)
THICKENED OR SOUR CREAM (I LIKE TO USE HALF AND HALF)	100 G (3½ OZ)
FRESCO CHEESE, COTIJA OR FETA, CRUMBLED	70 G (2½ OZ)
CORIANDER (CILANTRO) LEAVES, FINELY CHOPPED	70 G (2½ OZ)
SALSA ROJA (SEE PAGE 207)	TO SERVE
CHICHARRÓN PRENSADO	
PORK SKIN, CUT INTO 5 CM (2 IN) DICE	500 G (1 LB 2 OZ)
TABLE SALT	1 TABLESPOON
PORK LARD	500 G (1 LB 2 OZ)
EVAPORATED MILK	375 ML (12½ FL OZ)
CASTER (SUPERFINE) SUGAR	1 TEASPOON
DRIED GUAJILLO CHILLIES	3
WHITE ONION, ROUGHLY CHOPPED	½

To make the chicharrón prensado, rub the pork skin with the salt and let it rest for 10 minutes.

Heat the lard in a large saucepan over medium–high heat. Carefully add the salted pork skin, then reduce the heat to medium and cook, stirring frequently, for 5 minutes or until it starts to change colour. Slowly add the evaporated milk, followed by the sugar and continue to stir for 6–7 minutes until the pork skin is golden. Using a slotted spoon, remove the cooked pork skin and drain on a plate lined with paper towel. Set aside to cool for 10 minutes.

Place a square of plastic wrap over the bottom half of a tortilla press and place a cube of pork skin in the middle. Cover with another square of plastic wrap, then close the tortilla press and gently press to get rid of all the excess lard. Crumble the pork tortilla into a bowl, then repeat with the remaining pork skin.

Place the guajillo chillies and 500 ml (17 fl oz/2 cups) water in a saucepan, bring to the boil, then reduce the heat and simmer for 5 minutes. Set aside until cool enough to handle, then place the chillies in a blender with the cooking water and onion and blend to a chunky paste. Add the paste to the crumbled pork and mix well.

Heat enough vegetable oil for deep-frying in a large heavy-based saucepan to 180°C (350°F) on a kitchen thermometer. Take 100 g (3½ oz) of the tortilla dough and roll it into a ball. Gently flatten the ball into a thick tortilla no bigger than the size of your hand and place 50 g (1¾ oz) of the chicharrón prensado in the centre. Fold the tortilla over to enclose the filling and roll into a large ball. Flatten the ball slightly with your hands until it is about 12 cm (4¾ in) in diameter. Transfer the gordita to the hot oil and cook, flipping frequently, for 2–3 minutes, until light golden. Transfer to a plate lined with paper towel and repeat with the remaining tortilla dough and filling.

Prise open the gorditas and stuff with the onion, cream, cheese and coriander. Serve with salsa roja.

TLACOYOS

THICK OVAL TORTILLAS

I remember eating tlacoyos at the Friday street markets near my grandma's house, where a mother and daughter would sell them topped with cheese, chicharrón, broad beans or beans. The spicy sauce on top was always fresh and generous, while the blue corn and cactus salad made me think of Mexican recipes from long ago.

Here I've used black beans, but feel free to experiment with your favourite flavours and combinations. Do use blue masa flour if you can, but white or yellow masa flour will suffice if you can't get hold of any.

MAKES 6

TORTILLA DOUGH MADE WITH BLUE MASA FLOUR (SEE PAGE 196)	¾ x QUANTITY
FRIJOLES REFRITOS (SEE PAGE 53)	300 G (10½ OZ)
TOPPING	
TINNED NOPALES, SLICED INTO 3 CM x 1 CM (1¼ IN x ½ IN) STRIPS	500 G (1 LB 2 OZ)
TOMATOES, DICED	200 G (7 OZ)
WHITE ONION, DICED	50 G (1¾ OZ)
CORIANDER (CILANTRO) LEAVES	20 G (¾ OZ)
FRESCO CHEESE, COTIJA OR FETA, CRUMBLED	100 G (3½ OZ)
THICKENED CREAM	FOR DRIZZLING
SALSA TAQUERA (SEE PAGE 208; OPTIONAL)	TO SERVE

Take 100 g (3½ oz) of the tortilla dough and roll it into a ball. Using your hands, gently flatten the ball into a thick tortilla no bigger than the size of your hand. Place 50 g (1¾ oz) of the frijoles refritos in the centre of the tortilla, then fold the tortilla over to enclose the filling and roll into a large ball. Repeat with the remaining dough and frijoles refritos to make six balls.

Heat a comal or heavy-based frying pan over medium heat. Place a tortilla ball in the pan and use a spatula to flatten it into an 18 cm (7 in) oval with pointed ends. Cook the tlacoyo, flipping frequently, for 3 minutes, until light brown in spots. Remove from the pan and repeat with the remaining tortilla balls.

Meanwhile, combine the nopales, tomato, onion, coriander and cheese in a bowl. Spoon the topping onto the tlacoyos and finish with a drizzle of cream and a little salsa taquera (if using).

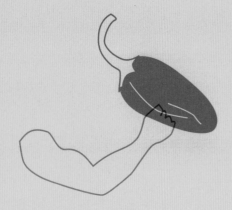

MOLOTES

This recipe comes from my mother's family. I remember visiting my relatives in a town called Agua Fria and my aunt Luz making molotes for all of us. During my last visit to Mexico I finally learned how to make them, and now I get to share the recipe in this book. I recommend using white or yellow masa flour as the contact with the hot oil brings out the flavour of the masa.

MAKES 15–20

VEGETABLE OIL	FOR DEEP-FRYING
TORTILLA DOUGH (SEE PAGE 196)	1 x QUANTITY
CHICKEN SALSA FILLING	
TOMATOES, ROUGHLY CHOPPED	3
WHITE ONION, ROUGHLY CHOPPED	½
GARLIC CLOVE	1
TABLE SALT	1 TABLESPOON
CHICKEN STOCK	350 ML (12 FL OZ)
GROUND CUMIN	PINCH
VEGETABLE OIL	3 TABLESPOONS
THYME, LEAVES PICKED	1 SMALL BUNCH
FINELY SHREDDED COOKED CHICKEN BREAST OR THIGHS	350 G (12½ OZ)
TOPPINGS	
SMALL ICEBERG LETTUCE, SHREDDED	1
THICKENED CREAM OR SOUR CREAM (I LIKE TO USE HALF AND HALF)	150 ML (5 FL OZ)
FRESCO CHEESE, COTIJA OR FETA, CRUMBLED	200 G (7 OZ)
SALSA ROJA (SEE PAGE 207)	TO SERVE

To make the chicken salsa filling, place the tomato, onion, garlic, salt, chicken stock and cumin in a food processor and blend to a chunky salsa.

Heat the oil in a frying pan over medium heat, add the salsa and cook, stirring frequently, for 7 minutes or until reduced and thick. Add the thyme and cook for a further 5 minutes, then remove from the heat and allow the salsa to cool to room temperature. Stir through the shredded chicken and set aside.

Heat the oil in a heavy-based frying pan over medium heat.

Roll 50 g (1¾ oz) of the tortilla dough into a ball. Using your hands, gently flatten the ball and add 1 tablespoon of the chicken salsa filling. Fold the dough over the filling to enclose, then roll the dough into an oval shape with pointy ends. Repeat with the remaining dough and filling to make 15–20 molotes.

Heat enough vegetable oil for deep-frying in a large heavy-based saucepan or deep-fryer to 180°C (350°F) on a kitchen thermometer. Working in small batches, fry the molotes for 4–5 minutes or until puffed up and lightly golden.

Transfer the molotes to a plate lined with paper towel to drain.

To serve, divide the molotes among shallow bowls and top with the lettuce, cream, cheese and salsa roja.

HUARACHES

These tortillas are named after the ancient Mexican sandal 'huarache' due to their long oblong shape. Served with a variety of toppings, I remember eating a very simple version in Mexico with my friend Cesar. The simplicity of the huarache enhanced the flavour of the black bean filling and salsa toppings, allowing me to savour every crispy bite. I've used white masa flour in this recipe, but you can also use yellow or blue masa flour if that's what you have.

MAKES 6

WHITE MASA FLOUR	500 G (1 LB 2 OZ)
WARM WATER	600 ML (20½ FL OZ)
TABLE SALT	LARGE PINCH
VEGETABLE OIL	100 ML (3½ FL OZ)
FRIJOLES REFRITOS (SEE PAGE 53)	300 G (10½ OZ)
LARD	1½ TABLESPOONS
TOPPINGS	
SALSA VERDE (SEE PAGE 206) AND SALSA ROJA (SEE PAGE 207)	TO SERVE
WHITE ONION, FINELY DICED	1
FRESCO CHEESE, COTIJA OR FETA, CRUMBLED	200 G (7 OZ)

Combine the masa flour, water, salt and oil in a bowl until the dough is soft and doesn't stick to your hands.

Roll 200 g (7 oz) of the dough into a ball, then press it into an oval shape no bigger than your hand. Make an indentation down the centre of the dough, so it resembles a shell. Place 50 g (1¾ oz) of the frijoles refritos in the centre, then carefully fold the dough to enclose the filling. The dough should now resemble a fat sausage.

Place a square of plastic wrap over the bottom half of an oval tortilla press (see Note). Place the dough in the middle of the tortilla press, then cover with another square of plastic wrap (this ensures the dough doesn't stick to the press). Close the tortilla press and gently press to flatten the dough into a 1 cm (½ in) thick oval. Try to stop any filling escaping, but you can patch it up with dough, if it does.

Heat 1 teaspoon of the lard in a comal or heavy-based frying pan over medium–low heat.

Open the tortilla press and lift out both sheets of plastic wrap containing the huarache. Peel back the top layer of plastic wrap and flip the huarache onto your hand. Peel off the bottom layer of plastic wrap and flip the huarache into the pan. Cook for 4 minutes on each side or until light golden and crisp. Repeat with the remaining dough and frijoles refritos.

Spoon the salsa verde onto one half of each huarache and the salsa roja on the other half. Scatter the diced onion over the top and finish with the cheese.

> **NOTE**
> If you don't have an oval tortilla press, don't worry! Just use a regular tortilla press and use a smaller quantity of dough and filling for each huarache.

GARNACHAS

TAC

EOS

TACOS TACOS TACOS

Todays tacos are a combination of Mexican and European ingredients, but the concept of placing a simple filling in a corn tortilla existed long before the arrival of the Spanish in the 16th century.

Tacos are incredibly diverse. In northern Mexico, where they rear the most meat, you'll find tacos de carne asada (see page 103) – tacos stuffed with marinated and grilled steak that are commonly served in flour tortillas instead of corn. If you head west to Mexico's Baja coast, you'll be rewarded with tortillas filled with seafood, including Baja's famous fish tacos. In central Mexico, the delicious and irresistible taco al pastor (see page 82), made with spit-grilled pork, is a firm favourite and combines European cooking techniques with local Mexican ingredients. Further down in Hidalgo, locals wrap whole lamb in agave leaves and slow-cook it in the ground until perfectly tender. The lamb is then served in tortillas with a simple lamb stock. Continue to Mexico's south, where you'll find cochinita pibil (pulled-pork) tacos, which are still made using Mayan cooking techniques dating back hundreds of years. Needless to say, wherever you go in Mexico, there will always be long queues at the local tortilleria – proof of the taco's enduring popularity and the symbolic relationship that Mexicans have with tortillas.

Thankfully, tacos are now so popular that they're sold in major cities all over the world. When I left Mexico to move to Australia, I realised just how much this simple food is celebrated and enjoyed by other cultures and communities. Mexican restaurants are now commonplace and even my local supermarket has a Mexican food section, which makes me proud of my cuisine and heritage. This familiarity helped me settle into my new home and was one of the main reasons I started to cook Mexican food in Australia, not only to share the love, but to teach people how to best use ingredients to make these authentic dishes outside of Mexico. This connection has helped me keep a small part of Mexico with me at all times, all through the power and love of food.

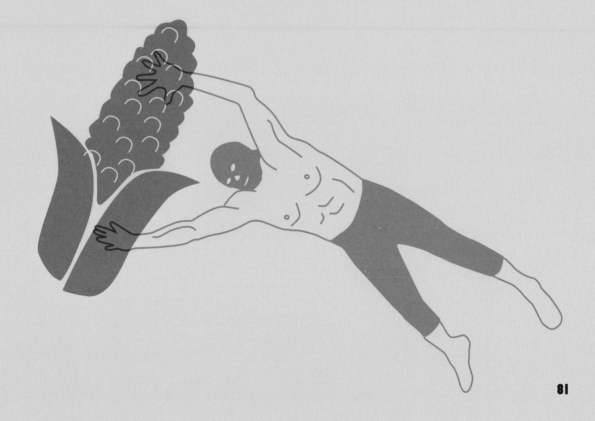

It is important to point out the difference between a tortilla and a taco as there is a common misconception that they are the same thing. A tortilla is the thin round corn base that holds any number of fillings. As soon as a filling is added to a tortilla it immediately becomes a taco.

In this chapter, I share some of Mexico's most popular tacos. They are authentic, homely, ridiculously tasty and perfect for sharing. Please give them a go the next time you have friends and family come to visit. You'll be glad you did!

TACOS AL PASTOR

Like many capital cities, Mexico City is a place where cultures and people collide, and nowhere is this collision more clearly seen than in the city's food. Tacos al pastor were the result of immigrants arriving from the Middle East in the 1960s, bringing with them lamb shawarma and gyros and, of course, the vertical grill. Once settled, the lamb was swapped for pork and beef, and Mexican spices and chillies, such as achiote and guajillo, were added. Pita breads became corn tortillas and a pineapple was added to the spit so the sweet juice could run down into the meat as it cooked.

Tacos al pastor are always served in double tortillas with finely chopped onion and coriander, freshly squeezed lime juice and spicy salsa.

MAKES 20

ACHIOTE PASTE	10 G (⅓ OZ)
DRIED GUAJILLO CHILLI POWDER	3½ TABLESPOONS
TABLE SALT	2 TEASPOONS
WHITE VINEGAR	50 ML (1¾ FL OZ)
BONELESS PORK LEG, CUT INTO 5 MM (¼ IN) THICK SLICES	1 KG (2 LB 3 OZ)
BEEF CHEEKS, CUT INTO 5 MM (¼ IN) THICK SLICES	500 G (1 LB 2 OZ)
WHITE ONIONS, THINLY SLICED	2
TORTILLA DOUGH (SEE PAGE 196)	2 x QUANTITIES
PINEAPPLE, PEELED, CORED, THINLY SLICED	¼
LIME WEDGES	TO SERVE
TOPPINGS	
WHITE ONION, DICED	1
CHOPPED CORIANDER (CILANTRO) LEAVES	25 G (¾ OZ)
SALSA TAQUERA (SEE PAGE 208)	300 ML (10½ FL OZ)

Place the achiote, chilli powder, salt and vinegar in the small bowl of a food processor and process to make a thick marinade.

Place the pork and beef cheek in a large bowl and rub the achiote marinade into the meat. Set aside in the fridge to marinate for at least 3 hours, but preferably overnight.

Preheat the oven to 180°C (350°F).

Place the marinated pork and beef in a roasting tin in a single layer and add the onion in between the slices of meat. Cover the tin with foil, then place in the oven and roast for 1 hour.

Meanwhile, make your tortillas! Follow the instructions on page 196 to make forty 11 cm (4¼ in) tortillas.

Remove the roasting tin from the oven and discard the foil. Place the pineapple over the pork and beef and return the tin, uncovered, to the oven and roast for a further 30 minutes.

Once the pastor is ready, slice the meat as thinly as you can (like shaved kebab meat) and divide it among 20 double-thickness tortillas.

Top the tacos with the onion, coriander, roasted pineapple and salsa taquera. Serve with lime wedges on the side.

TACOS DE SUADERO

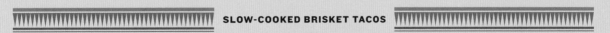

SLOW-COOKED BRISKET TACOS

Throughout Mexico, taco stalls offer a selection of mixed meat fillings which have been pre-prepared by the 'taquero' (taco seller). Every part of the animal is used, including intestines, head, eyes, cheeks, ears, tongue and brains. The tortillas are then heated in the same pan in the meat's juices to add flavour. Cold toppings might include spicy salsas, diced cucumber, sliced radish or black beans and, of course, a mango or guava 'boing' drink or a Mexican coke served alongside.

I remember the first time I prepared suadero using my dad's recipe. I made it for a Mexican community day in Sydney and my friend Carla, who claims to be my number one fan, had a long chat with me about how good the meat was and said I should start a business. I ended up taking her advice and today tacos de suadero are still one of my best-selling dishes.

MAKES 20

VEGETABLE OIL OR PORK LARD	150 ML (5 FL OZ)
BEEF BRISKET, CUT INTO 8–10 CM (3¼–4 IN) CHUNKS	1 KG (2 LB 3 OZ)
GARLIC CLOVE, MINCED	1
TABLE SALT	1 TEASPOON
FRESHLY SQUEEZED ORANGE JUICE	150 ML (5 FL OZ)
TORTILLA DOUGH (SEE PAGE 196)	2 x QUANTITIES
LIME WEDGES	TO SERVE
TOPPINGS	
WHITE ONION, DICED	1
CHOPPED CORIANDER (CILANTRO) LEAVES	25 G (¾ OZ)
LEBANESE (SHORT) CUCUMBERS, DICED	2
SALSA TAQUERA (SEE PAGE 208)	300 ML (10½ FL OZ)

Heat the oil or lard in a flameproof casserole dish over high heat. Add the brisket and sear for 10 minutes or until browned on all sides and the meat starts to release its juice. Add the garlic, salt, orange juice and 500 ml (17 fl oz/2 cups) water and stir to combine. Reduce the heat to medium, then cover and cook, stirring frequently, for 1½ hours or until the brisket is very tender.

If you like, heat a frying pan over high heat and sauté the cooked brisket for 5–7 minutes until crispy, but this step isn't crucial.

Allow the brisket to cool slightly, then cut into bite-sized pieces.

Meanwhile, make your tortillas! Follow the instructions on page 196 to make forty 11 cm (4¼ in) tortillas.

Divide the brisket among 20 double-thickness tortillas and top with the onion, coriander, cucumber and salsa taquera. Serve with lime wedges on the side.

TACOS DE CARNITAS

SLOW-COOKED PORK TACOS

My cousin Hugo taught me how to make carnitas during my last trip to Mexico. The original carnitas recipe comes from the state of Michoacán, but it's also a popular taco filling in Mexico City where locals eat tacos de carnitas for lunch.

Although a lot of people these days prefer to eat 'clean meat' (maciza), the only way to achieve the classic carnitas flavour is to add a little fat and a few greasy cuts, such as pork belly or ribs. Hugo recommends cooking carnitas in a copper saucepan, but you can use a regular pan if you don't have one.

MAKES 6

TABLE SALT	3 TABLESPOONS
PORK RIBS	250 G (9 OZ)
BONELESS PORK SHOULDER, CUT INTO 5 CM (2 IN) CHUNKS	1 KG (2 LB 3 OZ)
PORK BELLY, CUT INTO 5 CM (2 IN) CHUNKS	250 G (9 OZ)
PORK SKIN, CUT INTO 1 CM × 4 CM (½ IN × 1½ IN) STRIPS	100 G (3½ OZ)
PORK LARD	3 KG (6 LB 10 OZ)
EVAPORATED MILK	375 ML (12½ FL OZ)
ORANGE, CUT INTO 8 SLICES	1
COLA	500 ML (17 FL OZ/2 CUPS)
WHITE ONION	1
DRIED BAY LEAVES	6
FIZZY ORANGE SOFT DRINK	250 ML (8½ FL OZ/1 CUP)
DRIED THYME	1 TEASPOON
DRIED MARJORAM	1 TEASPOON
CLOVES	1 TABLESPOON
WHOLE PEPPERCORNS	1 TABLESPOON
GARLIC CLOVES	3
TORTILLA DOUGH (SEE PAGE 196)	½ × QUANTITY
TO SERVE	
PICO DE GALLO (SEE PAGE 205)	-
LIME WEDGES	-

Rub the salt into all the pork pieces and set aside.

Heat the pork lard in a large heavy-based saucepan over high heat to 120°C (240°F) on a kitchen thermometer.

Once the lard is hot, slowly add the evaporated milk, orange slices and cola, stirring to combine. Reduce the heat to medium, then add the onion, five of the bay leaves, the orange soft drink and 1 litre (34 fl oz/4 cups) water and stir again.

Tie the remaining bay leaf in a muslin bag with the thyme and marjoram and add this to the pan with the cloves, peppercorns and garlic. Continue to cook, stirring, for 5 minutes.

Add the ribs and pork shoulder and cook for 15 minutes, then add the pork belly. Cook, stirring frequently so the pork doesn't stick to the base of the pan, for 20–30 minutes, until the meat has a light golden crust. Add the pork skin and continue to simmer for 30 minutes or until tender.

Meanwhile, follow the instructions on page 196 to make six 16 cm (6¼ in) tortillas.

Remove the pork from the pan and set aside to cool slightly, then cut into small pieces. The pork should be tender and juicy.

Divide the carnitas among the tortillas and top with the pico de gallo. Serve with lime wedges on the side.

TACOS DE CHICHARRÓN EN SALSA VERDE

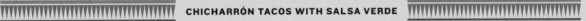

CHICHARRÓN TACOS WITH SALSA VERDE

Tacos de guisado are tacos filled with homely stews or braised meats. One of the most popular is the taco de chicharrón en salsa verde, which soaks and cooks crispy pork skin in the spicy green sauce. It's commonly eaten for breakfast in Mexico and taquerias will regularly run out by lunchtime. Whenever I visit Mexico City I always return to my favourite taco stall and order this taco. It's the perfect way to start the day.

MAKES 6

FRESH OR TINNED TOMATILLOS	500 G (1 LB 2 OZ)
WHITE ONION	½
FRESH JALAPENOS, CAYENNE OR SERRANO CHILLIES	3
CORIANDER (CILANTRO), LEAVES PICKED	1 BUNCH
TABLE SALT	1 TEASPOON
VEGETABLE OIL OR PORK LARD	2 TABLESPOONS
CHICHARRÓN	500 G (1 LB 2 OZ)
TORTILLA DOUGH (SEE PAGE 196)	½ x QUANTITY

If using fresh tomatillos, peel the husks and cut the tomatillos in half. If using tinned tomatillos, drain and rinse them.

Place the tomatillos in a saucepan with the onion, chillies, coriander, salt and 500 ml (17 fl oz/2 cups) water. Bring to the boil, then reduce the heat and simmer for 5 minutes. Drain, then transfer the ingredients to a blender and blend to make a smooth green salsa.

Heat the oil or lard in a frying pan over low heat for 3 minutes. Add the salsa and cook, stirring, for 5 minutes. Add the chicharrón and stir to combine with the salsa until it is soft and completely coated.

Meanwhile, follow the instructions on page 196 to make six 16 cm (6¼ in) tortillas.

Divide the chicharrón and salsa among the tortillas and serve.

TACOS DE CHICHARRÓN EN SALSA VERDE

TACOS DE CARNITAS

TACOS DE COCHINITA PIBIL

PULLED-PORK TACOS

Hailing from southern Mexico, cochinita pibil (Mexican pulled pork) is probably the most famous of all taco fillings. I always remember visiting our favourite family stall with Mum and Dad in Mexico City and struggling to choose between pulled-pork tortas, tacos, tostadas or panuchos. Do give this recipe a go – you'll be surprised at how easy it is to make.

MAKES ABOUT 10

ACHIOTE PASTE	150 G (5½ OZ)
WHITE VINEGAR	50 ML (1¾ FL OZ)
BITTER ORANGE JUICE (OR USE NORMAL ORANGE JUICE)	50 ML (1¾ FL OZ)
TABLE SALT	3 TEASPOONS
BONELESS PORK SHOULDER OR LEG, CUT INTO 5 CM (2 IN) CHUNKS	1 KG (2 LB 3 OZ)
TORTILLA DOUGH (SEE PAGE 196)	1 x QUANTITY
LIME WEDGES	TO SERVE
TOPPING	
RED ONION, JULIENNED	1
DRIED OREGANO	3 TEASPOONS
FRESHLY SQUEEZED LEMON JUICE	1 TEASPOON
TABLE SALT	PINCH
WHITE VINEGAR	1 TEASPOON

Place the achiote paste, vinegar, orange juice and salt in the small bowl of a processor and blend to a thick paste.

Place the pork in a large bowl and rub the achiote paste into the meat. Set aside in the fridge to marinate for at least 3 hours.

Preheat the oven to 220°C (430°F).

Place the marinated pork in a roasting tin in a single layer, cover with foil and roast for 1 hour.

Meanwhile, to make the topping, bring a small saucepan of water to the boil. Add the onion and blanch for 1 minute. Drain and immediately plunge the onion into a bowl of cold water to stop the cooking process. Drain again and place in a bowl with the oregano, lemon juice, salt and vinegar.

Remove the pork from the oven and discard the foil. Reduce the temperature to 150°C (300°F), return the pork to the oven and cook for a further 15 minutes.

Meanwhile, follow the instructions on page 196 to make twenty 11 cm (4¼ in) tortillas.

Using two forks, gently pull or shred the pork.

Divide the pulled pork among 10 double-thickness tortillas and top with the onion mixture. Serve immediately with lime wedges.

COOKWARE

Mexican cooking utensils are steeped in history and heritage, and although many were invented hundreds or even thousands of years ago, you will still find them in kitchens throughout the country. Here are some of the most popular.

Molcajete: Made from volcanic rock, this Mexican mortar and pestle is used to crush herbs, chillies and vegetables. The volcanic rock releases minerals that add a unique flavour to dishes.

Metate: A grinding stone also made from volcanic rock and one of the oldest domestic tools in Mexico. Metates always have three small legs to support the heavy flat stone that sits on top. It was traditionally used to grind corn into flour and can still be found remote in areas.

Comal: From clay to cast-iron, small to big, handmade or industrial, this flat griddle can be found in every Mexican kitchen, where it is used to heat tortillas, make quesadillas and much more. A heavy-based frying pan is a good alternative.

Jícara: A small wooden container traditionally made from the fruit of the calabash tree. Spoons and scoops have mostly replaced this ancient vessel, but you can still find beautifully carved and painted jícaras at some markets.

Tortilla press: An essential tool in any Mexican kitchen. There is nothing like a freshly made tortilla and while you can roll out the masa dough by hand, having a tortilla press enables you to make them faster and more consistent in size and shape. Tortilla presses can be purchased from most kitchenware shops.

Tamales steamer: A large deep steamer crucial for making tamales. They are easy to purchase at kitchenware shops. Alternatively, use a regular deep metal steamer.

TACOS DE LENGUA

The first time I ate tacos de lengua was when my mum brought them home and lied to me, saying they were carnitas. At the time, I was a very fussy eater and would never have tried an ox tongue taco! I completely fell in love with them and always visit my favourite lengua stall every time I go home to Mexico. Don't be put off by the ox tongue, as it makes a fantastic taco filling that's truly authentic. I highly recommend you try them and I promise you won't be disappointed.

MAKES 8

OX TONGUES	2
DRIED BAY LEAVES	10
WHOLE BLACK PEPPERCORNS	10
MARJORAM	2 SPRIGS
DRIED THYME	1 BUNCH
GARLIC CLOVES	4
WHITE ONION	½
TABLE SALT	3 TABLESPOONS
TORTILLA DOUGH (SEE PAGE 196)	1 x QUANTITY
LIME CHEEKS	TO SERVE
TOPPINGS	
WHITE ONION, DICED	½
CORIANDER (CILANTRO), LEAVES CHOPPED	1 BUNCH
SALSA TAQUERA (SEE PAGE 208)	300 ML (10½ FL OZ)

Wash the tongues, then place them in a large saucepan with the remaining ingredients except the tortillas. Bring to the boil over medium heat, then cover and simmer for 45 minutes or until tender.

Drain the tongues and set aside to cool slightly. Peel off the rough layer where the taste buds are, then chop the tongues into bite-sized pieces.

Meanwhile, follow the instructions on page 196 to make sixteen 11 cm (4¼ in) tortillas.

Divide the tongue among eight double-thickness tortillas and season with salt. Top with the onion, coriander and salsa taquera and serve with lime cheeks on the side.

TACOS DE CHORIZO

CHORIZO TACOS

Customers often ask me about Mexican chorizo and how it differs from its Spanish counterpart. Our chorizo is usually sold raw rather than cured and the meat is minced instead of chopped, resulting in a different consistency. We also add chillies rather than paprika to give it that distinctive red colour, which results in a more spicy sausage. In Mexico, we add chorizo to scrambled eggs and quesadillas or mix it through beans or potatoes. It's also a popular taco filling. Enjoy!

MAKES 20

DRIED GUAJILLO CHILLIES	3
DRIED BAY LEAVES	3
GROUND CUMIN	1½ TEASPOONS
DRIED OREGANO	1½ TEASPOONS
TABLE SALT	1 TEASPOON
GROUND CLOVES	1 TEASPOON
MINCED GARLIC	1 TEASPOON
GROUND CORIANDER	1 TEASPOON
FRESHLY GROUND BLACK PEPPER	1 TEASPOON
GROUND CINNAMON	½ TEASPOON
WHITE TEQUILA	30 ML (1 FL OZ)
WHITE VINEGAR	75 ML (2½ FL OZ)
MINCED (GROUND) FATTY PORK	750 G (1 LB 11 OZ)
MINCED (GROUND) PORK FAT	250 G (9 OZ)
TORTILLA DOUGH (SEE PAGE 196)	2 x QUANTITIES
TOPPINGS	
GUACAMOLE (SEE PAGE 204)	1 x QUANTITY
WHITE ONION, DICED	1
CHOPPED CORIANDER (CILANTRO) LEAVES	25 G (¾ OZ)

Place the guajillo chillies and bay leaves in a saucepan of cold water and bring to the boil. Boil for 5 minutes, then drain and transfer the chillies and bay leaves to a food processor. Add the cumin, oregano, salt, ground cloves, garlic, ground coriander, pepper, cinnamon, tequila and vinegar and process until well combined.

Transfer the mixture to a large bowl and add the minced pork and fat. Using your hands, massage the mixture into the meat until thoroughly combined. Cover and set aside in the fridge overnight.

Heat a comal or heavy-based frying pan over high heat. Add the chorizo mince and sauté for 10–15 minutes, until cooked through and starting to crisp.

Meanwhile, follow the instructions on page 196 to make forty 11 cm (4¼ in) tortillas.

Divide the chorizo mince among 20 double-thickness tortillas and top with the guacamole, onion and coriander.

TACOS DE LENGUA

TACOS DE CHORIZO

TACOS DE CANASTA

 **BASKET TACOS**

Tacos de canasta are a go-to dish for students, and they remind me of my college days when they were often the most affordable option. For this recipe, I highly recommend buying commercial tortillas instead of making them yourself as they need to be strong enough to hold the heavy filling, which is then covered with salsa.

MAKES 20

DRIED CASCABEL CHILLI	50 G (1¾ OZ)
WHITE ONION	½
MINCED GARLIC	1 TEASPOON
TABLE SALT	2 TEASPOONS
11 CM (4¼ IN) STORE-BOUGHT CORN TORTILLAS	20
FRIJOLES REFRITOS (SEE PAGE 53)	400 G (14 OZ)
SALSA VERDE (SEE PAGE 206)	TO SERVE

Place the cascabel chilli, onion and garlic in a small saucepan with 300 ml (10½ fl oz) water. Bring to the boil, then reduce the heat and simmer for 10 minutes.

Set aside to cool slightly, then transfer the mixture to a blender and blend with the salt until you have a runny, dark orange sauce. Transfer to a bowl.

Meanwhile, heat a comal or heavy-based frying pan over medium–high heat and cook the tortillas, flipping frequently, until soft and warmed through.

One by one, dip the warm tortillas in the cascabel sauce to coat on both sides.

Place the soaked tortillas on a chopping board and spoon 20 g (¾ oz) of the frijoles refritos onto each tortilla. Fold the tortillas in half and press the edges together with your fingertips. Transfer the folded tacos to a tortilla warmer, overlapping them, then pour the remaining cascabel sauce over the top.

Serve with salsa verde.

YAH!

TACOS DE CARNE ASADA

Carne asada tacos are the most popular tacos in northern Mexico which, perhaps not coincidentally, is also where most of the country's meat is produced. Even though I'm from Mexico City, we always have these tacos for Sunday lunch with family and friends. Don't forget to serve them with cold beer!

MAKES 12

SKIRT, FLANK OR RUMP STEAK	1 KG (2 LB 3 OZ)
MEXICAN BEERS	3 x 330 ML (11 FL OZ)
TABLE SALT	2 TABLESPOONS
FRESHLY GROUND BLACK PEPPER	1 TEASPOON
SPRING ONIONS (SCALLIONS)	12
TORTILLA DOUGH (SEE PAGE 196)	¾ x QUANTITY
TO SERVE	
GUACAMOLE (SEE PAGE 204)	-
PICO DE GALLO (SEE PAGE 205)	-
SALSA DE HABANERO Y PIÑA (SEE PAGE 212)	-
LIME WEDGES	-

Place the steak in a large bowl, pour over the beer and season with the salt and pepper. Stir to combine, then cover and set aside in the fridge overnight.

The next day, preheat a barbecue grill and flat plate to high. Place the spring onions on the flat plate and grill for 10 minutes or until slightly charred. Remove to a plate. Place the steak on the grill and cook for 3–4 minutes on both sides for medium–rare or until cooked to your liking. Remove the steak from the grill and rest for 5 minutes. Chop the steak into bite-sized pieces.

Meanwhile, follow the instructions on page 196 to make twelve 16 cm (6¼ in) tortillas.

Pile the steak into the tortillas and top with guacamole, pico de gallo and salsa de habanero y piña. Squeeze a lime wedge over the spring onions and season with salt. Serve alongside the tacos with extra lime wedges and cold beer!

TACOS DE BARBACOA

Tacos de barbacoa is an ancestral dish that uses an earth oven to slow-cook a whole lamb wrapped in agave leaves. Traditionally served with a consommé, there would always be enough food to feed the whole neighbourhood. In the cities, barbacoa stalls are particularly busy on weekend mornings when Mexicans are looking for a good hangover cure!

It's pretty hard to find agave leaves outside of Mexico, so I've used banana leaves here instead and even though the flavour is not quite the same, you won't be disappointed with the result.

MAKES ABOUT 10

BONELESS LAMB (A MIX OF LEG, SHOULDER AND SHANK), CHOPPED INTO CHUNKS	1 KG (2 LB 3 OZ)
TABLE SALT	80 G (2½ OZ)
MINCED GARLIC	1 TEASPOON
LARGE BANANA OR AGAVE LEAF	1
TORTILLA DOUGH (SEE PAGE 196)	½ x QUANTITY
LIME WEDGES	TO SERVE

TOPPINGS

WHITE ONION, DICED	½
CORIANDER (CILANTRO), LEAVES CHOPPED	1 BUNCH
GUACAMOLE (SEE PAGE 204)	200 G (7 OZ)
SALSA BORRACHA (SEE PAGE 214)	300 ML (10 FL OZ)

Place the meat in a bowl and rub with 3 tablespoons of the salt and the garlic.

Fill a large saucepan with 2 litres (68 fl oz/8 cups) water and add the remaining salt. Place a steamer basket on top and bring to a simmer.

Cut the banana or agave leaf into four 15 cm (6 in) squares and divide the meat among the leaves. Bring together the corners of each leaf and secure with kitchen string to make a pouch. Place the parcels in the steamer and cover.

Steam for 45 minutes, adding up to 1 litre (34 fl oz/4 cups) more water if the pan starts to dry out.

Unwrap the parcels and place the meat on a chopping board. Gently pull the lamb apart using two forks.

Meanwhile, follow the instructions on page 196 to make about ten 16 cm (6¼ in) tortillas.

Top each taco with the onion, coriander, guacamole and salsa borracha and serve with lime wedges on the side.

FLAUTAS

**ROLLED DEEP-FRIED
TACOS**

Flautas are filled and rolled tortillas which are deep-fried and served with a variety of toppings. They're a great way to use up left-over chicken, beef, lamb or veggies, but the most popular filling is always barbacoa. Make a double batch of the recipe opposite and use the leftovers to make these delicious fried tacos.

MAKES 12

TORTILLA DOUGH (SEE PAGE 196)	¾ x QUANTITY
VEGETABLE OIL	1 LITRE (34 FL OZ/4 CUPS)
BARBACOA (SEE OPPOSITE)	1 x QUANTITY
TOPPINGS	
ICEBERG LETTUCE, SHREDDED	½
TOMATOES, SLICED	3
THICKENED OR SOUR CREAM (I LIKE TO USE HALF AND HALF)	250 ML (8½ FL OZ/1 CUP)
AVOCADOS, SLICED	2
COTIJA OR FETA, CRUMBLED	100 G (3½ OZ)
SALSA DE CHIPOTLE (SEE PAGE 213)	TO SERVE

Follow the instructions on page 196 to make twelve 16 cm (6¼ in) tortillas. Warm the tortillas in a comal or heavy-based frying pan over medium heat.

Heat the oil in a large heavy-based saucepan or deep-fryer to 180°C (350°F) on a kitchen thermometer.

Meanwhile, divide the barbacoa evenly among the warm tortillas, then roll them up and secure with toothpicks.

Working in batches, deep-fry the flautas for 4–5 minutes, until crispy on both sides. Transfer to paper towel standing upright to drain the excess oil.

Remove the toothpicks and serve the flautas in pairs topped with the lettuce, tomato, cream, avocado, cheese and salsa de chipotle.

FLAUTAS

TACOS DE ALAMBRE

MEXICAN FAJITAS

Tacos de alambre combine carne asada with colourful bell peppers, chargrilled spring onions and Oaxaca cheese. Outside of Mexico they are commonly called fajitas.

MAKES 8

SKIRT, FLANK OR RUMP STEAK	1 KG (2 LB 3 OZ)
MEXICAN BEERS	3 x 330 ML (11 FL OZ)
TABLE SALT	2 TABLESPOONS
FRESHLY GROUND BLACK PEPPER	1 TEASPOON
RED BELL PEPPER (CAPSICUM), ROUGHLY CHOPPED	½
YELLOW BELL PEPPER (CAPSICUM), ROUGHLY CHOPPED	½
GREEN BELL PEPPER (CAPSICUM), ROUGHLY CHOPPED	½
SPRING ONIONS (SCALLIONS), TRIMMED AND HALVED LENGTHWAYS	8
STRINGED OAXACA CHEESE OR FIRM MOZZARELLA, GRATED	300 G (10½ OZ)
TORTILLA DOUGH (SEE PAGE 196)	½ x QUANTITY

TOPPINGS

GUACAMOLE (SEE PAGE 204)	150 G (5½ OZ)
PICO DE GALLO (SEE PAGE 205)	150 G (5½ OZ)
SALSA DE CHIPOTLE (SEE PAGE 213)	150 ML (5 FL OZ)
LIME WEDGES	TO SERVE

Place the steak in a large bowl and add the beer, salt and pepper. Stir to combine, then set aside in the fridge overnight.

Preheat a barbecue grill and flat plate to high.

Place the steak on the grill and cook for 3–4 minutes on both sides for medium–rare or until cooked to your liking. Place the bell peppers and spring onion on the flat plate and cook for 10 minutes, turning frequently, or until charred.

Remove the steak from the barbecue and let it rest for 5 minutes. Chop the steak into bite-sized pieces.

Heat a frying pan over medium heat and add the grilled steak, capsicum and cheese and cook, stirring, until the cheese has melted.

Meanwhile, follow the instructions on page 196 to make eight 16 cm (6¼ in) tortillas.

Divide the cheesy steak mixture among the tortillas and top with the spring onion, guacamole, pico de gallo and salsa de chipotle. Serve with lime wedges on the side.

TAM

TAMALES
TAMALES
TAMALES

Tamales are a culinary expression of dedication, patience, art and ancestral rituals all rolled into one. They are an integral part of Mexican cuisine that predate tortillas and there are over 400 registered recipes in Mexico. Tamales are sold by street vendors throughout Mexico and are wrapped either in corn husks or banana leaves and then steamed, boiled or baked.

Although time-consuming, don't be afraid of the labour involved as the process is wonderfully meditative and a great way to get family and friends involved. Most of the recipes in this chapter are easy to make and celebrate some of Mexico's most popular tamale fillings. The tamale dough recipe comes from my father and it forms the base of my signature dish at my tamaleria.

Dried corn husks can be purchased online or from Mexican supermarkets. You can also use fresh corn husks, but these can be more fiddly as you need to keep the husks intact when removing them from the corn. Banana leaves for Oaxaca-style tamales are easier to source. Just make sure they are clean and wilted before using them.

Tamale steamers are relatively easy to find online and at some kitchenware shops. Alternatively, you can use a large metal steamer, but avoid bamboo steamers as they are not efficient for cooking the masa. When steaming tamales, add enough water to reach the base of the steamer and keep a jug of water near by to top up the water level as needed. Layer the base of the steamer with banana leaves or corn husks, then add another layer on top of your tamales followed by a tea towel to help prevent steam escaping and water dripping back down on the tamales. I also recommend placing a heavy object on top of the lid as the tamales will expand, causing the lid to pop off and water to escape.

Finally, to make tamales, I recommend that you are in a good mood without stress or anxiety, and preferably around people you love with your favourite music playing in the background. In Mexico, we truly believe that if you are in a bad mood or have cried during that day, the dough will never float, which means your tamales won't cook properly.

TAMALES VERDES

In Mexico, tamales verdes are the most popular of all tamales. They are also a bestseller at my tamaleria in Sydney. Tamales verdes can be made with pork or chicken and with a spicy or mild sauce. Making tamales is a process of love. It hope you enjoy it!

MAKES 10

SWEETCORN HUSKS (SEE NOTE)	20
PORK LARD	200 G (7 OZ)
BAKING POWDER	1 TEASPOON
MASA FLOUR, SIFTED	500 G (1 LB 2 OZ)
TABLE SALT	2 TEASPOONS
CHICKEN STOCK, WARMED	650 ML (22 FL OZ)
COOKED SHREDDED CHICKEN BREAST OR THIGHS	500 G (1 LB 2 OZ)
SALSA VERDE (SEE PAGE 206)	500 ML (17 FL OZ / 2 CUPS)

Soften the sweetcorn husks in water, then drain to remove any excess water.

Place the lard and baking powder in a bowl and whip the mixture as fast as possible using a wooden spoon – the lard needs to soften and look spongy. Don't stress if this takes a long time; it can take up to 15 minutes to achieve the right consistency, especially if this is the first time you're making tamales. Once the lard is ready, add the flour, salt and warm chicken stock and mix well until completely combined. To test if the dough is ready, drop a small ball of dough into a cup of cold water; if it floats to the top you're good to go!

Spread 80 g (2¾ oz) of the dough in the middle of a damp sweetcorn husk, leaving a 4 cm (1¼ in) border around the edge. Add 50 g (1¾ oz) of the shredded chicken, 50 ml (1¾ fl oz) of the salsa verde, then cover with another 20 g (¾ oz) of dough. Place another sweetcorn husk over the filling, then wrap up the tamale by overlapping the sides and folding over the top and bottom edges towards the centre to enclose the filling. Secure the ends with kitchen string and set aside. Repeat with the remaining husks and ingredients to make 10 tamales.

Place the tamales standing upright in a large steamer (do not stack on top of each other). Fit as many tamales as you can into the steamer, but be careful not to pack them in too tightly as they can burst, leaving you with empty tamales. Place the steamer over a saucepan of simmering water and steam for 45 minutes.

The best way to check if your tamales are cooked is to remove one from the steamer, let it cool for 5 minutes and then unwrap the husks. If the masa doesn't stick to the husks and looks shiny and fluffy, then your tamales are ready.

Leave the tamales to cool for 15–20 minutes inside the steamer, then transfer to serving plates and serve.

NOTE
You can buy dried sweetcorn husks from Latin American supermarkets or online.

TAMALES DE RAJAS

**POBLANO CHILLI
TAMALES**

Tamales de rajas are by far my favourite tamale to eat in Australia. The rich poblano chilli flavour combined with cheese and salsa de chipotle makes them truly unique. I regularly ate these when I first started making tamales, and even though this isn't an original recipe from the streets of Mexico, it is a thoroughly delicious interpretation made using ingredients readily available at any Latin American supermarket.

MAKES 10

SWEETCORN HUSKS (SEE NOTE OPPOSITE)	20
PORK LARD	100 G (3½ OZ)
VEGETABLE SHORTENING, SOFTENED	100 G (3½ OZ)
BAKING POWDER	1 TEASPOON
MASA FLOUR, SIFTED	500 G (1 LB 2 OZ)
TABLE SALT	2 TEASPOONS
CHICKEN STOCK, WARMED	500 ML (17 FL OZ/2 CUPS)
POBLANO CHILLIES, THINLY SLICED	500 G (1 LB 2 OZ)
FIRM MOZZARELLA, SHREDDED	250 G (9 OZ)
SALSA DE CHIPOTLE (SEE PAGE 213)	500 ML (17 FL OZ/2 CUPS)

Soften the sweetcorn husks in water, then drain to remove any excess water.

Place the lard, vegetable shortening and baking powder in a bowl and whip the mixture as fast as possible using a wooden spoon – the lard needs to soften and look spongy. Don't stress if this takes a long time; it can take up to 15 minutes to achieve the right consistency, especially if this is the first time you're making tamales. Once the lard is ready, add the flour, salt and warm chicken stock and mix well until completely combined. To test if the dough is ready, drop a small ball of dough into a cup of cold water; if it floats to the top you're good to go!

In a bowl, combine the poblano chilli, mozzarella and salsa de chipotle.

Spread 80 g (2¾ oz) of the dough in the middle of a damp sweetcorn husk, leaving a 4 cm (1¼ in) border around the edge. Add 80 g (2¾ oz) of the poblano filling, then cover with another 20 g (¾ oz) of dough. Place another sweetcorn husk over the filling, then wrap up the tamale by overlapping the sides and folding over the top and bottom edges towards the centre to enclose the filling. Secure the ends with kitchen string and set aside. Repeat with the remaining husks and ingredients to make 10 tamales.

Place the tamales standing upright in a large steamer (do not stack on top of each other). Fit as many tamales as you can into the steamer, but be careful not to pack them in too tightly as they can burst, leaving you with empty tamales. Place the steamer over a saucepan of simmering water and steam for 45 minutes.

The best way to check if your tamales are cooked is to remove one from the steamer, let it cool for 5 minutes and then unwrap the husks. If the masa doesn't stick to the husks and it looks shiny and fluffy, then your tamales are ready.

Leave the tamales to cool for 15–20 minutes inside the steamer, then transfer to serving plates and serve.

TAMALES

TAMALES VERDES

TAMALES DE RAJAS

TAMALES DE MOLE

MOLE TAMALES

Mole is a very rich and dense sauce traditionally made with dried chillies, nuts, spices and Mexican chocolate. There are many varieties throughout Mexico, but the most common for making tamales is the poblano mole from the state of Puebla. This mole has a long list of ingredients and it's not a sauce that many Mexican people would normally make from scratch. If you feel the same way, you can easily purchase a good-quality commercial brand, such as Dona Maria, online or from your local Latin American supermarket.

MAKES 10

SWEETCORN HUSKS (SEE NOTE ON PAGE 114)	20
COOKED SHREDDED CHICKEN BREAST OR THIGHS	500 G (1 LB 2 OZ)
TAMALE VERDE DOUGH (SEE PAGE 114)	1 x QUANTITY
MOLE	
PEPITAS (PUMPKIN SEEDS)	100 G (3½ OZ)
SESAME SEEDS	30 G (1 OZ)
WHOLE CLOVES	1 TABLESPOON
SULTANAS (GOLDEN RAISINS)	30 G (1 OZ)
CINNAMON STICKS	5
RAW ALMONDS	4
VEGETABLE OIL	200 ML (7 FL OZ)
PLANTAIN, PEELED AND CHOPPED INTO CHUNKS	1
BOLILLO (MEXICAN BREAD ROLL), OR CRUSTY ROLL CUT INTO CHUNKS	½
GARLIC CLOVES, ROUGHLY CHOPPED	10
LARGE WHITE ONION, ROUGHLY CHOPPED	1
PECANS	16
UNSALTED RAW PEANUTS	30 G (1 OZ)
WHOLE BLACK PEPPERCORNS	1 TABLESPOON
MEXICAN ABUELITA OR IBARRA CHOCOLATE BAR	1
DRIED MULATO CHILLIES	250 G (9 OZ)
DRIED ANCHO CHILLIES	500 G (1 LB 2 OZ)
MARIE (RICH TEA) BISCUITS	250 G (9 OZ)
DEEP-FRIED CORN TORTILLA (SEE PAGE 27)	1
PORK LARD	250 G (9 OZ)
CHICKEN STOCK OR WATER	2 LITRES (68 FL OZ/8 CUPS)

Although time-consuming, it is important to cook the mole ingredients separately as some take longer than others and any overcooked ingredients will result in a bitter-tasting dish.

Firstly, place the pepitas in a comal or heavy-based frying pan and toast, stirring, over medium heat for 4–5 minutes or until lightly golden. Set aside on a plate. Now repeat this process for the sesame seeds, cloves and sultanas, toasting each ingredient separately and transferring to the plate with the pepitas. Add the cinnamon sticks to the pan and toast for 10 minutes.

Meanwhile, boil the almonds in water for 5 minutes. Drain and set aside.

Heat the oil in a frying pan over medium heat. Add the plantain and bolillo and cook, stirring, for 7 minutes or until golden. Remove from the pan and set aside on a plate, then add the garlic and cook for 5 minutes. Add the garlic to the cooked plantain, then cook the onion for 5 minutes before also transferring to the plate with the plantain and garlic.

Transfer all the toasted and cooked ingredients to a food processor and add the remaining mole ingredients except the pork lard and stock or water. Blitz them all together to make a paste.

Heat the pork lard in a large saucepan over medium heat. Add the mole paste and cook, stirring, for 10 minutes. Add the chicken stock or water and cook, stirring, for 1½ hours or until the mole is reduced and thick.

Meanwhile, soften the sweetcorn husks in water, then drain to remove any excess water.

Place the chicken in a large bowl and stir through half the mole sauce.

Spread 80 g (2¾ oz) of the tamale dough in the middle of a damp sweetcorn husk, leaving a 5 cm (2 in) border around the edge. Add 50 g (1¾ oz) of the mole chicken, then cover with 50 ml (1¾ fl oz) of the mole sauce and another 20 g (¾) of dough. Place another

sweetcorn husk over the filling, then wrap up the tamale by overlapping the sides and folding over the top and bottom edges towards the centre to enclose the filling. Secure the ends with kitchen string and set aside. Repeat with the remaining husks and ingredients to make 10 tamales.

Place the tamales standing upright in a large steamer (do not stack on top of each other). Fit as many tamales as you can into the steamer but be careful not to pack them in too tightly as they can

burst, leaving you with empty tamales. Place the steamer over a saucepan of simmering water and steam for 45 minutes. The best way to check if your tamales are cooked is to remove one from the steamer, let it cool for 5 minutes and then unwrap the husks. If the masa doesn't stick to the husks and it looks shiny and fluffy, then your tamales are ready.

Leave the tamales to cool for 15–20 minutes inside the steamer, then transfer to serving plates and serve.

TAMALES OAXAQUEÑOS DE MOLE NEGRO

BLACK MOLE TAMALES

Mole negro is one of the seven moles of Oaxaca. It has a strong taste with quite a kick, especially if you're not used to eating chillies or spicy food. Chilhuacle negro, rojo, mulato and pasilla chillies are just some of the ingredients used to make this delicious sauce, which is the favourite mole for Oaxacan locals. Chilhuacle chillies are hard to find outside of Oaxaca, so for this recipe I recommend purchasing a mole negro sauce online, such as Mayordomo. Tamales Oaxaqueños are wrapped in banana leaves and usually filled with chicken.

MAKES 10

VEGETABLE OIL	1 TABLESPOON
BLACK MOLE PASTE, SUCH AS MOLE NEGRO MAYORDOMO	200 G (7 OZ)
CHICKEN STOCK OR WATER	1 LITRE (34 FL OZ/4 CUPS)
TAMALES VERDE DOUGH (SEE PAGE 114)	1 x QUANTITY
15 CM (6 IN) SQUARE BANANA LEAVES, PLUS EXTRA IN CASE THEY BREAK OR SPLIT	10
COOKED SHREDDED CHICKEN BREAST OR THIGHS	500 G (1 LB 2 OZ)
SALSA VERDE (SEE PAGE 206) AND SALSA DE CHIPOTLE (SEE PAGE 213)	TO SERVE

Heat the oil in a saucepan over medium heat. Add the black mole paste and chicken stock or water and stir until combined. Simmer until reduced to 500 ml (17 fl oz/2 cups) of mole sauce.

Spread 100 g (3½ oz) of the tamale dough in the middle of a banana leaf to make a rectangle, leaving a 5 cm (2 in) border around the edge. Add 50 g (1¾ oz) of the chicken, then cover with 50 ml (1¾ fl oz) of the mole sauce. Wrap up the banana leaf, so the filling is completely enclosed and secure with kitchen string. Repeat with the remaining banana leaves and ingredients to make 10 tamales.

Stack all but one tamale in a steamer one on top of the other with the folded edges facing upwards. Place the last tamale with the folded edges facing down to stop the banana leaf unfolding.

Place the steamer over a saucepan of simmering water and steam for 45 minutes.

The best way to check if your tamales are cooked is to remove one from the steamer, let it cool for 5 minutes and then unwrap the banana leaf. If the masa doesn't stick to the leaf and it looks shiny and fluffy, then your tamales are ready.

Leave the tamales to cool for 15–20 minutes inside the steamer, then transfer to serving plates and serve with salsa verde and salsa de chipotle on the side.

TAMALES DE DULCE

Sweet tamales might not sound very traditional, but there have always been tamale vendors located in certain corners of Mexico City who specialise in them. They have gained popularity in recent years and the variety of fillings has grown to include Mexican chocolate, avocado, crème caramel, blackberry and cheese among others. These sultana tamales, however, are definitely a classic!

MAKES 10

SWEETCORN HUSKS (SEE NOTE ON PAGE 114)	20
PORK LARD	200 G (7 OZ)
BAKING POWDER	2 TEASPOONS
CASTER (SUPERFINE) SUGAR	400 G (14 OZ)
MASA FLOUR, SIFTED	500 G (1 LB 2 OZ)
SULTANAS (GOLDEN RAISINS)	200 G (7 OZ)
PINK FOOD COLOURING	1 TEASPOON
WARM WATER	400 ML (13½ FL OZ)
STRAWBERRIES	TO SERVE

Soften the sweetcorn husks in water, then drain to remove any excess water.

Place the lard, baking powder and sugar in a bowl and whip the mixture as fast as possible using a wooden spoon – the lard needs to soften and look spongy. Don't stress if this takes a long time; it can take up to 15 minutes to achieve the right consistency, especially if this is the first time you're making tamales. Once the lard is ready, add the flour and sultanas. Whisk together the pink food colouring and warm water, then add to the dough and mix well until completely combined.

Spread 200 g (7 oz) of the dough in the middle of a damp sweetcorn husk, leaving a 5 cm (2 in) border around the edge. Place another sweetcorn husk over the filling, then wrap up the tamale by overlapping the sides and folding over the top and bottom edges towards the centre to enclose the filling. Secure the ends with kitchen string and set aside. Repeat with the remaining husks and dough to make 10 tamales.

Place the tamales standing upright in a large steamer (do not stack on top of each other). Fit as many tamales as you can into the steamer but be careful not to pack them in too tightly as they can burst, leaving you with empty tamales. Place the steamer over a saucepan of simmering water and steam for 45 minutes.

The best way to check if your tamales are cooked is to remove one from the steamer, let it cool for 5 minutes and then unwrap the husks. If the masa doesn't stick to the husks and it looks shiny and fluffy, then your tamales are ready.

Leave the tamales to cool for 15–20 minutes inside the steamer, then transfer to serving plates and serve with fresh strawberries on the side.

TAMALES DE PIÑA

PINEAPPLE TAMALES

Tamales de piña are classic sweet tamales from northern Mexico. In addition to pineapple, they are commonly filled with nuts and rompope (an egg nog–like drink) or even made with apple and cinnamon. I've gone for a more simple version here, using only pineapple chunks and the syrup from the tin. They are still completely delicious, and the perfect hot dessert to serve with Mexico's famous café de olla or a pecan atole.

MAKES 10

SWEETCORN HUSKS (SEE NOTE ON PAGE 114)	20
PORK LARD	200 G (7 OZ)
BAKING POWDER	2 TEASPOONS
CASTER (SUPERFINE) SUGAR	400 G (14 OZ)
MASA FLOUR, SIFTED	500 G (1 LB 2 OZ)
FINELY DICED TINNED PINEAPPLE IN SYRUP	200 G (7 OZ)
YELLOW FOOD COLOURING	1 TEASPOON
PINEAPPLE SYRUP FROM THE TIN	400 ML (13½ FL OZ)

Soften the sweetcorn husks in water, then drain to remove any excess water.

Place the lard, baking powder and sugar in a bowl and whip the mixture as fast as possible using a wooden spoon – the lard needs to soften and look spongy. Don't stress if this takes a long time; it can take up to 15 minutes to achieve the right consistency, especially if this is the first time you're making tamales. Once the lard is ready, add the flour and pineapple. Whisk together the yellow food colouring and pineapple syrup, then add to the lard mixture and mix well until completely combined.

Spread 200 g (7 oz) of the dough in the middle of a damp sweetcorn husk, leaving a 5 cm (2 in) border around the edge. Place another sweetcorn husk over the filling, then wrap up the tamale by overlapping the sides and folding over the top and bottom edges towards the centre to enclose the filling. Secure the ends with kitchen string and set aside. Repeat with the remaining husks and dough to make 10 tamales.

Place the tamales standing upright in a large steamer (do not stack on top of each other). Fit as many tamales as you can into the steamer but be careful not to pack them in too tightly as they can burst, leaving you with empty tamales. Place the steamer over a saucepan of simmering water and steam for 45 minutes.

The best way to check if your tamales are cooked is to remove one from the steamer, let it cool for 5 minutes and then unwrap the husks. If the masa doesn't stick to the husks and it looks shiny and fluffy, then your tamales are ready.

Leave the tamales to cool for 15–20 minutes inside the steamer, then transfer to serving plates and serve.

TAS

TORTAS
TORTAS
TORTAS

I rate tortas in the top five street foods of Mexico City! Perhaps best described as a giant sandwich, tortas are convenient, versatile and cheap, making them extremely popular with locals and visitors alike.

Tortas can be served cold with very simple fillings, but the best-loved interpretations are grilled (a la plancha) and stacked high with myriad meats, cheeses, salads and salsas, such as the famous Torta Cubana (see page 134), which is filled with every ingredient at the torteria (sandwich shop).

Street vendors specialise in particular fillings, which locals regularly return to for their lunchtime sandwich fix. The recipes in this chapter celebrate Mexico's most popular tortas, but, of course, these recipes are just a guide and I encourage you to experiment with your own combinations, using what you love and have to hand. There really are no rules when it comes to tortas!

Tortas are so big, they are often considered a complete meal in their own right. The fillings are stuffed into a 'telera', a large crusty white roll not dissimlar to French bread in terms of lightness and taste, but with a rounded shape to enable it to hold more ingredients. The interior soft white bread or 'migajon' is also usually removed to make more room for the filling.

The base of nearly all torta fillings is a spread of butter, followed by a large spoon of refried beans, sliced tomato, onion and avocado. For a heat kick, some vendors will add pickled jalapenos or chipotle chillies in adobo sauce. When it comes to protein, the options are endless and may include egg, sausage, Mexican chorizo, pastor (spit-grilled pork), pork steak, ham, head cheese, veal schnitzel, octopus, beef brisket or grilled chicken. The protein is then topped with Oaxaca cheese, manchego, Swiss or American cheese, or pineapple.

Out of all the Mexican dishes I love, tortas will forever be my favourite. It is the meal I miss most and is the first and last thing I eat every time I visit Mexico.

TORTA DE MILANESA CON QUESILLO Y CHILE CHIPOTLE

**SCHNITZEL TORTA WITH
CHEESE AND CHIPOTLE**

Out of all of Mexico's sandwiches, torta de milanesa is undoubtedly the best. I often dream of visiting my favourite torta stall in Mexico and devouring this giant sandwich, which is extremely hard to eat because of its ridiculous size. It's super easy to make and you can swap out any of the ingredients with your favourite fillings – just grill and layer them up.

MAKES 1

LARGE TELERA (TORTA ROLL) OR FRENCH ROLL	1
UNSALTED BUTTER	1 TEASPOON
WHOLE-EGG MAYONNAISE	2 TABLESPOONS
FRIJOLES REFRITOS (SEE PAGE 53)	2 TABLESPOONS
AVOCADO, MASHED	1
TOMATO, SLICED	1
WHITE ONION, SLICED	¼
TABLE SALT	PINCH
STRINGED OAXACA, MANCHEGO, PANELA OR AMERICAN CHEESE, SHREDDED	50 G (1¾ OZ)
PICKLED JALAPENOS OR CHOPPED CHIPOTLE CHILLIES IN ADOBO SAUCE	TO TASTE
VEAL SCHNITZEL	
FREE-RANGE EGG, LIGHTLY BEATEN	1
FULL-CREAM (WHOLE) MILK	150 ML (5½ FL OZ)
TABLE SALT	1 TEASPOON
FRESHLY GROUND BLACK PEPPER	PINCH
VEAL MINUTE STEAK	1
DRIED BREADCRUMBS	100 G (3½ OZ/1 CUP)
VEGETABLE OIL	50 ML (1¾ FL OZ)

To make the veal schnitzel, combine the egg, milk, salt and pepper in a bowl. Add the veal and soak for 3 minutes.

Place the breadcrumbs in another bowl, then add the soaked veal and press the breadcrumbs into the steak, making sure it's completely covered on both sides.

Heat the oil in a frying pan over medium–high heat, add the schnitzel and cook for 2–3 minutes on each side until crisp and cooked through. Place the schnitzel on a plate lined with paper towel to drain, then slice into 3 cm (1¼ in) wide strips. Wipe out the frying pan.

Slice the bread roll in half. Spread the butter on one side and mayonnaise on the other side.

Heat the frying pan over low heat, then place the buttered half of the roll butter side down in the pan, and the other half of the roll mayonnaise side up in the pan. Once the buttered half is lightly toasted, flip it over and spread the frijoles refritos over the top. Lightly toast, then remove both roll halves from the pan. Spread the avocado over the mayonnaise and top with the tomato, onion and salt.

Preheat a grill (broiler) to high. Sprinkle the cheese over the veal schnitzel.

Grill the schnitzel and cheese until the cheese melts (the cooking time will depend on the kind of cheese you are using: American cheese melts quicker than Oaxaca cheese, for example), then pile the cheesy schnitzel on top of the onion and add pickled jalapenos or chipotle chilli to taste.

Close the roll halves together so you have one giant torta and dig in!

TORTA CUBANA

CUBAN TORTA

Torta Cubana is Mexico's biggest and best-selling torta, and one that I can never finish by myself. It's made with all the ingredients on the torta stall, so make sure you use a large telera or French roll as your base and have lots of napkins handy to mop up the huge mess you're about to make.

MAKES 1

VEGETABLE OIL	2 TEASPOONS
FREE-RANGE EGGS, LIGHTLY BEATEN	2
LARGE TELERA (TORTA ROLL) OR FRENCH ROLL	1
UNSALTED BUTTER	1 TABLESPOON
WHOLE-EGG MAYONNAISE	2 TABLESPOONS
FRIJOLES REFRITOS (SEE PAGE 53)	1 TABLESPOON
AVOCADO, MASHED	1
TOMATO, SLICED	½
WHITE ONION, THINLY SLICED	¼
TABLE SALT	PINCH
HAM SLICES	6
VEAL SCHNITZEL (SEE PAGE 133), SLICED	1
SLICED ROAST PORK	50 G (1¾ OZ)
STRINGED OAXACA CHEESE	20 G (¾ OZ)
MANCHEGO CHEESE, SLICED	20 G (¾ OZ)
AMERICAN CHEESE, SLICED	20 G (¾ OZ)
AMERICAN MUSTARD (OPTIONAL)	FOR DRIZZLING
PICKLED JALAPENOS OR CHOPPED CHIPOTLE CHILLIES IN ADOBO SAUCE	TO TASTE

Heat the oil in a small frying pan over medium–high heat. Add the beaten egg and swirl to coat the base of the pan, then cook for 1–2 minutes until the egg starts to set. Fold the omelette in half, cook for a few more seconds, then remove from the pan and set aside.

Slice the bread roll in half. Spread the butter on one side and the mayonnaise on the other side.

Heat a frying pan over low heat. Place the buttered half of the roll butter side down in the pan, and the other half of the roll mayonnaise side up in the pan. Once the buttered half is lightly toasted, flip it over and spread the frijoles refritos over the top. Lightly toast, then remove both roll halves from the pan. Spread the avocado over the mayonnaise and top with the tomato, onion and salt.

Preheat a grill (broiler) to high.

Layer the meat and cheese on top of each other, then grill until the cheese starts to melt. Scoop the meat and melted cheese onto the onion and top with the omelette. Drizzle with mustard (if using) and add pickled jalapenos or chipotle chilli, to taste. Close the roll halves together and devour.

TEQUILA AND MEZCAL

Legend has it that after the fall of the Aztec empire, a field of agave plants was struck by lightning, setting the agave on fire. All that remained were the cores of the plants, which the locals harvested and cooked. The result was a rich, sweet juice that, when fermented and distilled, became aguardiente, a beverage that literally means 'water that burns'.

It is said that the first tequilas were so harsh that people started to put salt on their hands and a few drops of lime in their mouths to help them swallow it, a technique which any tequila drinker will be familiar with. Today, tequila is big business, with aged, high-end tequilas that should only ever be sipped and savoured becoming increasingly available.

Mezcal is another distilled alcohol extracted from the agave plant. Wrongly considered by many as a cheap drink, mezcal has an earthy, smoky flavour, and in recent times its popularity has soared, with high-quality mezcal now considered to be one of the great drinks of the world. It is known as the cleanest spirit available, as mezcal can only be made from 100 per cent agave. This results in minimal hangovers, which is surely something to celebrate. In some parts of Mexico, mezcal is served with orange wedges and worm or grasshopper salt. The salt is made by grinding the worms or grasshoppers found in the leaves of the agave plant into a powder, which is then combined with salt and chilli. Some mezcal brands add a whole worm to the bottle and it's considered lucky if you get the chance to eat it!

TORTA DE JAMÓN CON QUESO

HAM AND CHEESE TORTA

The most commonly sold torta on the streets of Mexico, this ham and cheese sandwich is for many Mexicans their go-to lunch. Served hot or cold, these tortas appear in school lunchboxes all over the country and no family road trip is complete without Mexican mums carrying this ubiquitous snack in their handbags for inevitably bored and hungry kids. I remember buying tortas de jamón con queso from our local cornershop when I walked past every day on my way to school. I never missed the chance to buy one for the bus trip; they were small but delicious!

MAKES 1

LARGE TELERA (TORTA ROLL) OR FRENCH ROLL	1
UNSALTED BUTTER	1 TABLESPOON
WHOLE-EGG MAYONNAISE	2 TABLESPOONS
FRIJOLES REFRITOS (SEE PAGE 53)	1 TABLESPOON
AVOCADO , MASHED	1
TOMATO, SLICED	1
WHITE ONION, SLICED	¼
TABLE SALT	PINCH
DRIED OREGANO (OPTIONAL)	PINCH
HAM SLICES	6
STRINGED OAXACA, OR SLICED MANCHEGO, PANELA OR AMERICAN CHEESE	50 G (1¾ OZ)
AMERICAN MUSTARD (OPTIONAL)	FOR SPREADING
PICKLED JALAPENOS OR CHOPPED CHIPOTLE CHILLIES IN ADOBO SAUCE	TO TASTE

Slice the bread roll in half. Spread the butter on one side and the mayonnaise on the other side.

Heat a frying pan over low heat. Place the buttered half of the roll butter side down in the pan, and the other half of the roll mayonnaise side up in the pan. Once the buttered half is lightly toasted, flip it over and spread the frijoles refritos over the top. Lightly toast, then remove both roll halves from the pan. Spread the avocado over the mayonnaise and top with the tomato, onion, salt and oregano (if using).

Preheat a grill (broiler) to high.

Layer the ham and cheese and grill until the cheese starts to melt. Place on top of the onion and add the mustard (if using) and pickled jalapenos or chipotle chilli, to taste.

Close the roll halves together and dig in.

TORTAS

TORTAS DE COCHINITA PIBIL

 **PULLED-PORK TORTAS**

Tortas de cochinita pibil are not commonly sold at torta stalls in Mexico; instead you will always find them at the local cochinita pibil (pulled pork) taco stall. Compared to other tortas, this sandwich is small in size, but don't let that fool you as it's big on flavour from the amazing pork and pickled red onion. Oh, and don't forget to add habanero salsa for an extra kick!

MAKES 4

TELERAS (TORTA ROLLS) OR FRENCH ROLLS	4
FRIJOLES REFRITOS (SEE PAGE 53)	200 G (7 OZ)
COCHINITA PIBIL (SEE PAGE 92)	1 KG (2 LB 3 OZ)
PICKLED RED ONION (SEE PAGE 92)	80 G (2¾ OZ)
SALSA DE HABANERO Y PIÑA (SEE PAGE 212)	80 G (2¾ OZ)
DRIED OREGANO	PINCH

Cut the rolls in half and spread both sides of each roll with the frijoles refritos.

Heat a frying pan over medium heat. Working in batches, place the rolls cut side down in the pan and toast until the beans form a crust. Turn the rolls over and divide the cochinita pibil among the bottom halves of the rolls.

Remove the rolls from the pan and place the pickled red onion, salsa and oregano on top of the cochinita pibil.

Close the rolls together and serve.

TORTA DE JAMÓN CON QUESO

TORTAS DE COCHINITA PIBIL

TORTA HAWAIANA

HAWAIIAN TORTA

Kids love torta Hawaiana! Pineapple is a popular fruit in Mexico that pops up in all sorts of dishes. Its sweet, fresh flavour appeases even the fussiest of eaters and it can always be found at the local torta stall.

MAKES 1

TELERA (TORTA ROLL) OR FRENCH ROLL	1
UNSALTED BUTTER	1 TABLESPOON
WHOLE-EGG MAYONNAISE	2 TABLESPOONS
FRIJOLES REFRITOS (SEE PAGE 53)	1 TABLESPOON
AVOCADO, MASHED	1
TOMATO, SLICED	½
WHITE ONION, SLICED	¼
TABLE SALT	PINCH
HAM SLICES	6
STRINGED OAXACA OR SLICED MANCHEGO, PANELA OR AMERICAN CHEESE	50 G (1¾ OZ)
TINNED PINEAPPLE SLICES IN SYRUP, DRAINED	2
PICKLED JALAPENOS OR CHOPPED CHIPOTLE CHILLIES IN ADOBO SAUCE (OPTIONAL)	TO TASTE

Slice the bread roll in half. Spread the butter on one side and mayonnaise on the other side.

Heat a frying pan over low heat. Place the buttered half of the roll butter side down in the pan, and the other half of the roll mayonnaise side up in the pan. Once the buttered half is lightly toasted, flip it over and spread the frijoles refritos over the top. Lightly toast, then remove both roll halves from the pan. Spread the avocado over the mayonnaise and top with the tomato, onion and salt.

Preheat a grill (broiler) to high.

Layer the ham and cheese and grill until the cheese starts to melt, then top with the pineapple slices and grill for another couple of minutes. Pile the mixture onto the onion and top with pickled jalapenos or chipotle chilli (if using).

Close the roll halves together and enjoy.

TORTAS DE CHILAQUILES

TORTILLA CHIP TORTAS

There is a very famous torta stall in Mexico City where the torta de chilaquiles was born. Chilaquiles are basically tortilla chips cooked in salsa and they are one of Mexico's favourite hangover cures. They were originally eaten with a bread roll on the side, but one day someone came up with the idea of serving the chilaquiles INSIDE the roll and the results were amazing! Filled with your favourite protein, tortas de chilaquiles are a must-try if you visit Mexico. Alternatively, follow this recipe and bring Mexico to your table!

MAKES 6

SALSA VERDE (SEE PAGE 206)	1 LITRE (34 FL OZ/4 CUPS)
TOTOPOS (SEE PAGE 27) OR STORE-BOUGHT TORTILLA CHIPS, LIGHTLY CRUSHED	1 KG (2 LB 3 OZ)
TELERAS (TORTA ROLLS) OR FRENCH ROLLS	6
THICKENED OR SOUR CREAM (I LIKE TO USE HALF AND HALF)	30 G (1 OZ)
COTIJA OR FETA, CRUMBLED	30 G (1 OZ)
VEAL SCHNITZELS (SEE PAGE 133), SLICED	6

Heat all but 3 tablespoons of the salsa verde in a saucepan over medium heat. Throw in the totopos and add 250 ml (8½ fl oz/1 cup) water. Cook, stirring frequently, for 5 minutes or until the salsa verde is heated through. Remove the chilaquiles from the heat.

Cut the rolls in half and divide the chilaquiles among the rolls. Drizzle the cream over the top and scatter in the cheese. Add the veal schnitzel, drizzle in the remaining salsa verde, then close the rolls together and serve.

TORTA DE SUADERO

**SLOW-COOKED
BRISKET TORTA**

I first ate a torta de suadero when my mum brought one home for dinner from our local taco stall. Suadero is a popular taco filling in Mexico, but the idea of putting it in a torta was genius. It combines two of my favourite foods and it's the perfect solution if you can't decide between a taco and a sandwich. Enjoy!

MAKES 1

TELERA (TORTA ROLL) OR FRENCH ROLL	1
SUADERO COOKING FAT (SEE PAGE 85)	2 TEASPOONS
SUADERO (SEE PAGE 85)	250 G (9 OZ)
CHOPPED WHITE ONION	25 G (¾ OZ)
CHOPPED CORIANDER (CILANTRO) LEAVES	25 G (¾ OZ)
LIME, JUICED	½
SALSA TAQUERA (SEE PAGE 208)	TO SERVE

Cut the roll in half and spread the suadero cooking fat over the cut surface.

Heat a frying pan over low heat and place the roll cut side down in the pan. Move the roll to one side, add the suadero and cook, stirring, until heated through. Scoop the suadero onto the bottom half of the roll and top with the onion, coriander and lime juice. Spoon in a generous helping of salsa taquera, then close the roll together and serve.

SEA

OOD

SEAFOOD
SEAFOOD
SEAFOOD

Mexico's vast coastline offers up a huge variety of seafood, which is transformed into regional specialties, such as delicious fish tacos from Baja, amazing zarandeado (grilled/broiled fish with chilli) from Nayarit and pescado a la Veracruzana – a simple dish of fish cooked in tomatoes, capers and olives.

Spending time on the Mexican coast is a must for anyone visiting the country, not only to soak up the beautiful beaches with their soft sands, rolling waves and palm trees, but also to experience the local seafood on offer and spend time with the locals who are always happy to recommend their favourite dishes and most popular restaurants, where chefs cook up their signature recipes using fresh and locally sourced ingredients, all washed down with a cold beer or a cocktail.

In addition to restaurants, food vendors walk up and down the beaches selling seafood tacos and quesadillas, along with snacks, tamales, sweets, fruit, fresh drinks and more, meaning you don't even have to leave the comfort of your beach towel and that breathtaking view to enjoy

a simple and beautiful meal that's come straight from the ocean.

The immense array of Mexican seafood dishes couldn't possibly fit in one book, so in this chapter I've selected a few of the most popular that are sold throughout Mexico and made with easy-to-find ingredients.

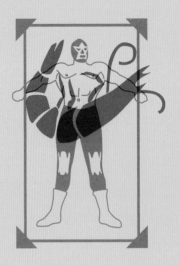

PESCADITOS

Pescaditos are very popular in Mexico City, but you will only find them at the local markets and certainly not all year round. The best way to enjoy them is with freshly squeezed lime juice and Valentina hot sauce.

SERVES 6

GARLIC POWDER	1 TEASPOON
SALT AND PEPPER	TO TASTE
FIRM WHITE SKINLESS FISH FILLETS, CUT INTO 12 STRIPS	1 KG (2 LB 3 OZ)
CANOLA OIL	FOR DEEP-FRYING
LIMES, HALVED	3
VALENTINA HOT SAUCE	TO SERVE
BATTER	
PLAIN (ALL-PURPOSE) FLOUR	110 G (4 OZ/¾ CUP)
BAKING POWDER	1 TEASPOON
TABLE SALT	½ TEASPOON

Combine the batter ingredients and 185 ml (6½ fl oz/¾ cup) water to reach a pancake consistency, then set aside at room temperature for 30 minutes. Whisk again to fully incorporate the ingredients.

Sprinkle the garlic powder, salt and pepper over the fish.

Heat enough oil for deep-frying in a large heavy-based saucepan or deep-fryer to 180°C (350°F) on a kitchen thermometer.

Dip the fish strips into the batter until completely coated then, working in batches, fry the fish for 5 minutes or until golden and crisp. Drain on a plate lined with paper towel, then transfer to a serving dish.

Serve with the lime halves for squeezing over and a good drizzle of Valentina hot sauce.

CEVICHE

Making Mexican-style ceviche reminds me of busy marisquerias (seafood restaurants), where family and friends come together to enjoy regional fish dishes and enjoy the local 'jarocho' band in a bid to recreate a beach atmosphere in a busy city where there's little opportunity to escape to the coast for a holiday. Fresh fish cooked in lime with a twist of fresh veggies and chilli is one of the best dishes to eat on a hot summer's day!

SERVES 4

SKINLESS BARRAMUNDI FILLETS OR ANY FIRM WHITE FISH FILLETS, CUT INTO 5 CM (2 IN) CHUNKS	1 KG (2 LB 3 OZ)
FRESHLY SQUEEZED LIME JUICE	500 ML (17 FL OZ/2 CUPS)
TOMATOES, DICED	500 G (1 LB 2 OZ)
WHITE ONION, DICED	150 G (5½ OZ)
CORIANDER (CILANTRO) LEAVES, CHOPPED	150 G (5½ OZ)
FRESH JALAPENO, GREEN CAYENNE OR SERRANO CHILLIES, DESEEDED AND FINELY CHOPPED	50 G (1¾ OZ)
EXTRA VIRGIN OLIVE OIL	1 TEASPOON
AVOCADO, HALVED AND SLICED	1
TO SERVE	
CORIANDER (CILANTRO) LEAVES	–
SALADA CRACKERS	–
LIME WEDGES	–

Place the fish and lime juice in a non-reactive bowl and set aside in the fridge overnight.

The next day, drain the fish and chop it into small bite-sized pieces. Return the fish to the bowl and add the tomato, onion, coriander, chilli and olive oil.

Divide the ceviche among four serving glasses and top with the avocado. Garnish with coriander sprigs, and serve with salada crackers and lime wedges on the side.

Bam!

Bam!

TOSTADAS DE CAMARÓN

PRAWN TOSTADAS

A good seafood stall will always have tostadas de camaron. My dad used to take us all to Coyoacán, a municipality in Mexico City, to eat a huge range of tostadas at the local market, where one stall in particular was celebrated for its prawn tostadas. Here is the recipe. I hope you love them as much as I do.

MAKES 10

COOKED PEELED MEDIUM PRAWNS (SHRIMP)	1 KG (2 LB 3 OZ)
PICO DE GALLO (SEE PAGE 205)	700 G (1 LB 9 OZ)
AVOCADOS, DICED	2
OLIVE OIL	1 TABLESPOON
WHOLE-EGG MAYONNAISE	150 G (5½ OZ)
FRESHLY MADE TOSTADAS (SEE PAGE 62)	10

Set aside 20 prawns, then cut the remaining prawns into bite-sized pieces.

Combine the chopped prawn, pico de gallo, avocado and olive oil in a bowl.

Spread 1 tablespoon of mayonnaise onto each tostada, then top with the prawn mixture and finish with two whole prawns. Serve immediately.

TOSTADAS DE JAIBA

CRAB TOSTADAS

I first tried tostadas de jaiba with my parents at the same market in Coyoacán in Mexico City. The flavour and combination of crisp, freshly fried tostadas, rich, decadent crab and Thousand Island dressing was unforgettable, so I had to recreate the recipe for this book. Eat them in summer with ice-cold beer.

MAKES 10

FRESHLY PICKED OR TINNED CRAB MEAT	1 KG (2 LB 3 OZ)
PICO DE GALLO (SEE PAGE 205)	700 G (1 LB 9 OZ)
AVOCADOS, DICED	2
LEBANESE (SHORT) CUCUMBERS, DICED	2
THOUSAND ISLAND DRESSING	150 ML (5 FL OZ)
FRESHLY MADE TOSTADAS (SEE PAGE 62)	10
CORIANDER (CILANTRO) LEAVES	TO SERVE

Combine the crab meat, pico de gallo, avocado and cucumber in a bowl.

Spread 1 tablespoon of Thousand Island dressing onto each tostada, then top with the crab mixture. Decorate with coriander leaves and serve.

COCTEL DE CAMARÓN

You can find coctel de camarónes at markets throughout Mexico, and it is the most popular seafood dish in Mexico City. Served either with salada crackers or totopos, this prawn cocktail is the perfect refreshment on a hot, sticky day in the city.

SERVES 6

COOKED PEELED SMALL PRAWNS (SHRIMP)	1 KG (2 LB 3 OZ)
PICO DE GALLO (SEE PAGE 205)	700 G (1 LB 9 OZ)
CLAMATO JUICE	500 ML (17 FL OZ/2 CUPS)
TOMATO KETCHUP	100 ML (3½ FL OZ)
AVOCADO, SLICED	1
TO SERVE	
CORIANDER (CILANTRO) LEAVES	–
LIME WEDGES	–
SALADA CRACKERS	–

Combine the prawns, pico de gallo, clamato juice and tomato ketchup in a bowl.

Divide the prawn mixture among six serving glasses and top with the avocado. Garnish with a few coriander leaves and serve with lime wedges and saladas on the side.

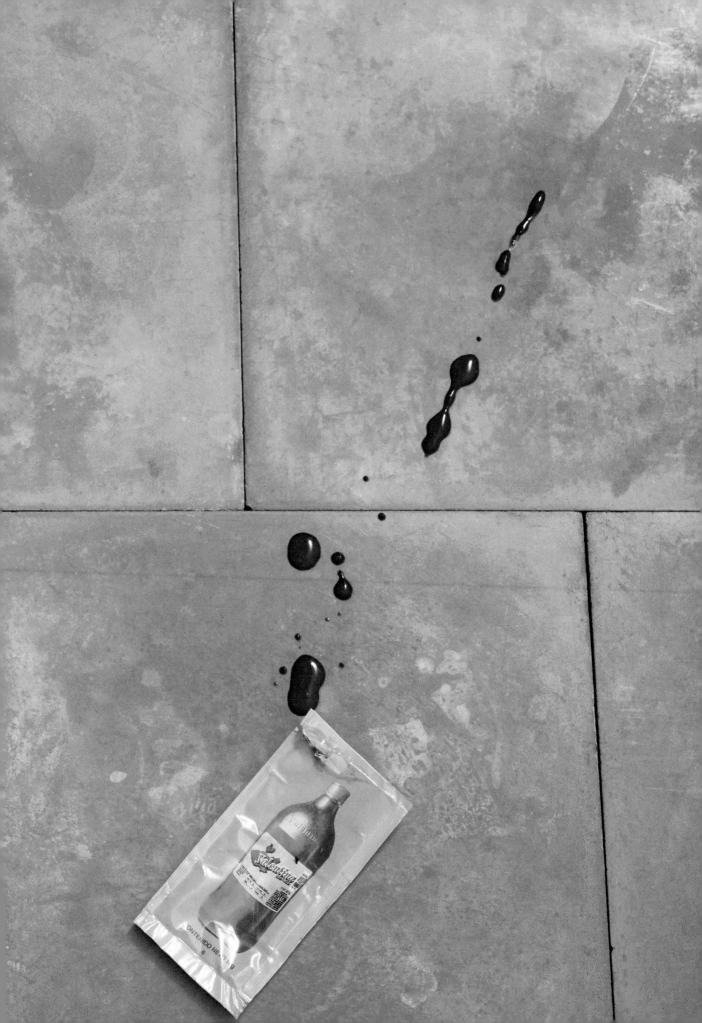

EMPANADAS DE ATUN

TUNA EMPANADAS

In Mexico, freshly made empanadas are sold at 'panaderias' (bakeries) morning, noon and night. Perfect for feeding a crowd and with a range of fillings, they are a popular, cheap and tasty snack that everyone loves. This recipe comes from my mum, so, of course, I think it's the best. It also makes a great taco filling. Tuna empanadas are traditionally eaten at Easter but I personally like to enjoy them all year round!

MAKES 20

VEGETABLE OIL	2 TABLESPOONS
WHITE ONION, DICED	1
MINCED GARLIC	1 TEASPOON
TINNED TUNA, DRAINED	500 G (1 LB 2 OZ)
SALSA DE CHIPOTLE (SEE PAGE 213)	350 ML (12½ FL OZ)
DRIED OREGANO	PINCH
FROZEN PUFF PASTRY, JUST THAWED	5 SHEETS
FREE-RANGE EGGS, LIGHTLY BEATEN	2
GUACAMOLE (SEE PAGE 204)	TO SERVE

Heat the oil in a frying pan over medium heat. Throw in the onion and garlic and cook for 3 minutes. Add the tuna and stir for 1 minute. Add the salsa de chipotle and continue to cook, stirring frequently, for 5 minutes or until heated through. Stir through the oregano, then remove the pan from the heat, cover and set aside for 1 hour.

Preheat the oven to 200°C (400°F). Line a large baking tray with baking paper.

Drain the tuna mixture to remove the excess liquid (we need it to be as dry as possible).

Cut each pastry sheet into four 12 cm (4¾ in) circles, then divide the tuna mixture evenly among the pastry circles.

Fold the pastry in half over the filling, brushing the edges with the beaten egg to help them stick. Use a fork to crimp and secure the pastry edges, then brush the tops with beaten egg.

Transfer the empanadas to the prepared baking tray and bake in the oven for 15–20 minutes, until golden and crisp.

SEAFOOD

EMPANADAS DE CAMARÓN

PRAWN EMPANADAS

I love empanadas de camarónes from Veracruz, and I fondly remember visiting with my friend Gil who knew exactly where to get the best ones! In Veracruz they are called volovanes and you will often see vendors at traffic lights selling these delicious pastries from handbaskets covered with a tea towel. This recipe, however, belongs to my dad and it's what we eat every Easter week in Sydney.

MAKES 20

RED BELL PEPPER (CAPSICUM), SLICED	400 G (14 OZ)
STORE-BOUGHT BECHAMEL SAUCE	500 G (1 LB 2 OZ)
SALT AND PEPPER	TO TASTE
VEGETABLE OIL SPRAY	FOR COOKING
COOKED AND PEELED SMALL PRAWNS (SHRIMP), DICED	500 G (1 LB 2 OZ)
FROZEN PUFF PASTRY, JUST THAWED	5 SHEETS
FREE-RANGE EGGS, LIGHTLY BEATEN	2

Place the bell pepper, bechamel sauce, salt and pepper in a blender and blend until smooth.

Spray a frying pan with oil spray and place over medium heat. Add the bell pepper and bechamel sauce and cook for 2 minutes or until heated through. Add the prawn and stir for 1 minute, then remove from the heat, cover and set aside for 1 hour.

Preheat the oven to 200°C (400°F). Line a large baking tray with baking paper.

Cut each pastry sheet into 12 cm (4¾ in) circles, then divide the prawn mixture evenly among the pastry circles.

Fold the pastry in half over the filling, brushing the edges with the beaten egg to help them stick. Use a fork to crimp and secure the pastry edges, then brush the tops with beaten egg.

Transfer the empanadas to the prepared baking tray and bake in the oven for 15–20 minutes, until golden and crisp.

EMPANADAS

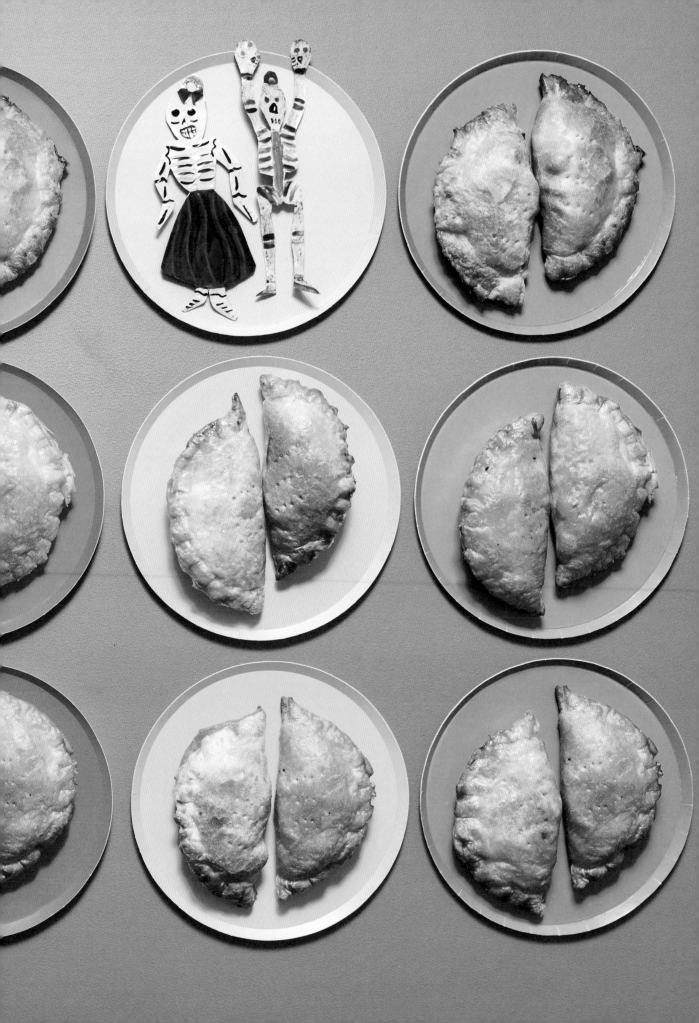

DESS

ERTS

DESSERTS
DESSERTS
DESSERTS

It is true to say that most Mexicans have an extremely sweet tooth! This love affair with sweets and desserts dates back to pre-Hispanic times and can be attributed to the wealth of sweet indigenous ingredients our country is blessed with. Sap from the maguey plant (a relative of the agave plant) and honey-pot ants, along with fruit pulps, nuts, seeds and even cactus were all used by the Aztecs to create sweet treats.

At that time, chocolate was only consumed as a bitter drink (although it was deemed so valuable it was also used as a currency), but with the arrival of the Spanish and sugar cane, the cocoa bean was transformed into the sweetened version we all know and love today. Nowadays, indigenous sweeteners have been replaced with brown or unrefined cane sugar (piloncillo), but if you are lucky you might still find delicacies made with these traditional ingredients in remote areas.

One ancient dish that is easy to find is alegrias, a candied bar made with amaranth seeds. Although now sweetened with cane sugar, it is still close to the original and no Mexican cookbook would be complete without a recipe, which you will find on page 178.

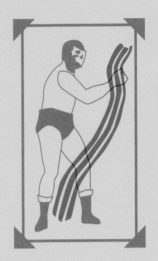

With the arrival of the Spanish and Christianity, convents became the unlikely home of many of Mexico's more modern confectionary and nuns would combine local and imported ingredients to create new sweets, such as marzipan, caramels, cookies and stuffed sweet limes (see page 177). Of course, no Mexican dessert chapter would be complete without the much-loved street snack, churros (see page 174) and a celebration cake, Mexican style, topped with fresh cream and fruit.

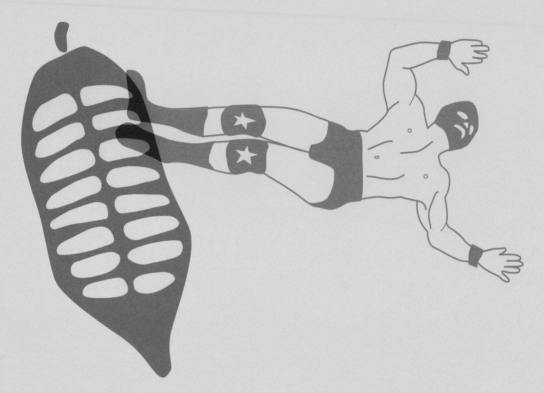

CHURROS

Sold by street-food vendors throughout the day, churros are a favourite snack to indulge in while wandering Mexico's city streets. Simply dusted in cinnamon sugar or stuffed with chocolate or dulce de leche, churros are nearly always accompanied by coffee, hot chocolate or the Mexican masa drink atoles. In winter, restaurants and cafes put out signs advertising churros to entice customers in to enjoy these deep-fried doughnuts served with a warming bowl of melted chocolate. I remember going to our local churros place three blocks from my grandma's house, where a huge churros machine churned out lengths of dough into even bigger deep-fryers of bubbling oil that cooked the churros and gave them their distinctive crunch and soft pillowy centre.

MAKES 15

PLAIN (ALL-PURPOSE) FLOUR	250 G (9 OZ)
TABLE SALT	1 TEASPOON
VEGETABLE OIL	1 LITRE (34 FL OZ/4 CUPS)
CASTER (SUPERFINE) SUGAR	100 G (3½ OZ)
GROUND CINNAMON	30 G (1 OZ)

Place the flour in a large bowl.

Heat 250 ml (8½ fl oz/1 cup) water in a small saucepan to 60°C (140°F) on a kitchen thermometer. Stir through the salt, then pour the water into the flour. Use a wooden spoon to combine the ingredients until you have a hard, sticky dough. Set aside to cool for 5 minutes, then transfer the dough to a piping bag fitted with a 2.5 cm (1 in) star nozzle.

Heat the oil in a large heavy-based saucepan or deep-fryer to 180°C (350°F) on a kitchen thermometer.

Working in batches, pipe approximately 10 cm (4 in) lengths of the dough into the hot oil and fry for 2 minutes or until brown and crisp. Using a slotted spoon, transfer the churros to a plate lined with paper towel to soak up any excess oil.

Combine the sugar and cinnamon on a plate, then roll the hot churros in the mixture to coat. Serve immediately while still warm.

LIMONES RELLENOS DE COCO

COCONUT-STUFFED LIMES

I love limones rellenos! They're fresh, sweet, sour and thoroughly addictive. When I was young, my family and I would go out for tacos and at the end of the meal I would sneak outside and find the ladies selling desserts from their baskets. I would always buy the limones rellenos.

I have been making them myself for many years; they are easy to put together and you can find the ingredients at any supermarket. Outside of Mexico, limes can be expensive, so I recommend waiting until you're making a dish that requires lots of lime juice as we're only using the shells here.

MAKES 24

LIMES	12
GREEN VEGETABLE COLOURING	4 DROPS
SHREDDED COCONUT	250 G (9 OZ)
CASTER (SUPERFINE) SUGAR	50 G (1¾ OZ)

Cut the limes in half and scoop out the pulp. Place the lime halves in a saucepan with plenty of water and bring to the boil over medium heat. Boil for 10 minutes to soften the skins, then remove from the heat.

Add the green vegetable colouring to the pan and set aside for 5 minutes. Drain, then place the limes on a plate and set aside in the fridge for 10 minutes to dry out.

In a separate saucepan, combine the shredded coconut, sugar and 250 ml (8½ fl oz/1 cup) water and place over low heat. Cook, stirring, for 7 minutes or until the mixture is sticky.

Carefully spoon the coconut mixture into the lime halves and serve.

ALEGRIAS

AMARANTH CANDIES

Amaranth is a popular grain in Mexico due to its rich flavour and health-giving properties. It is one of the main ingredients of alegrias, handmade treats decorated with nuts and sultanas that are sold at metro stations and by vendors at traffic lights. Alegrias are also traditionally made for Día de Muertos (Day of the Dead) celebrations where amaranth skulls are decorated and presented as gifts at the numerous alters throughout the country. Feel free to mix up the nuts, seeds and fruit in this recipe and use whatever you have in your pantry.

MAKES 24

227 G (4½ OZ) PILONCILLO BAR (OR 200 G/7 OZ CANE SUGAR)	1
AMARANTH SEEDS	1 KG (2 LB 3 OZ)
RAW PECAN HALVES	10
UNSALTED RAW PEANUTS	1 TABLESPOON
PEPITAS (PUMPKIN SEEDS)	1 TABLESPOON
SULTANAS (GOLDEN RAISINS)	1 TABLESPOON

Place the piloncillo bar or cane sugar and 250 ml (8½ fl oz/1 cup) water in a saucepan over medium heat and cook, stirring, for 15 minutes or until you have a sticky syrup. Set aside to cool until warm.

Line a 20 cm x 10 m (8 in x 4 in) loaf (bar) tin with baking paper.

Place the amaranth in a bowl, then pour over the syrup and stir until completely combined. Spoon the amaranth mixture into the prepared tin and use a spatula to press the mixture into an even layer without any holes. Top with the nuts, seeds and fruit and gently press them into the amaranth mixture. Set aside for at least 2 hours to set.

Cut the alegrias into 24 slices and serve.

FLAN MEXICANO

MEXICAN FLAN

Like other countries, the origin of Mexican flan comes from the classic French crème caramel. I have eaten flans from South America and even Asia and it's incredible to see just how similar they all are in flavour and texture, even though the ingredients might be quite different. Thankfully, Mexican flan uses easy-to-find ingredients and is quicker to make than other styles. Just let it cool and it's ready to serve.

SERVES 10

CASTER (SUPERFINE) SUGAR	115 G (4 OZ)
CONDENSED MILK	395 ML (13½ FL OZ)
EVAPORATED MILK	375 ML (12½ FL OZ)
FREE-RANGE EGGS	5
VANILLA ESSENCE	1 TABLESPOON
CAJETA (SEE NOTE; OPTIONAL)	FOR DRIZZLING

Preheat the oven to 50°C (120°F). Place a 23 cm (9 in) round cake tin in the oven to heat up.

Combine the sugar and 1 tablespoon water in a small saucepan over medium heat and cook, stirring, for 6–7 minutes, until you have a dark-golden caramel.

Remove the cake tin from the oven and carefully pour the caramel over the base of the tin. Set aside to cool for 20 minutes. Increase the oven temperature to 180°C (350°F).

Combine the milks, eggs and vanilla in a blender and blitz until smooth, then pour the mixture into the cake tin. Cover with foil, then transfer to the oven and bake for 45 minutes or until just set.

Remove the flan from the oven, discard the foil and allow the flan to cool for 20 minutes before transferring to the fridge for 1–2 hours or, preferably, overnight.

Run a knife around the edge of the flan, then very carefully invert it onto a large serving plate. Cut into slices, drizzle with cajeta (if using) and serve.

NOTE

Cajeta is a type of dulce de leche. You will find it at Latin American supermarkets.

CAPIROTADA

I first tried capirotada in Sydney when my dad prepared it as an offering for our Día de Muertos (Day of the Dead) celebrations. It was a huge hit and many of our friends came away with the recipe to recreate at home. In Mexico, this rich, seasonal dessert is popular during Lent when it is sold on the streets and at the weekly markets, but it is also made for Sunday lunch if there's a special request. The fresh cheese sprinkled throughout the layers perfectly balances the sweetness of the dish, making it impossible to stop at just one piece.

SERVES 6

227 G (4½ OZ) PILONCILLO BAR (OR 200 G/7 OZ CANE SUGAR)	1
CINNAMON STICK	1
WHOLE CLOVES	2
VEGETABLE OIL, PLUS EXTRA FOR GREASING	3 TABLESPOONS
BOLILLOS (MEXICAN BREAD ROLLS) OR FRENCH ROLLS, CUT INTO 3 CM (1¼ IN) THICK SLICES	2
UNSALTED RAW PEANUTS	20 G (¾ OZ)
SULTANAS (GOLDEN RAISINS)	20 G (¾ OZ)
COTIJA OR FETA, CRUMBLED	200 G (7 OZ)

Place the piloncillo bar or cane sugar, cinnamon, cloves and 375 ml (12½ fl oz/1½ cups) water in a small saucepan and bring to the boil over medium heat. Cook, stirring, for 10 minutes or until you have a runny caramel. Set aside to cool until warm.

Preheat the oven to 120°C (250°F). Lightly grease a small baking dish.

Brush the oil on both sides of the bread slices, then spread out in a single layer on a baking tray and toast in the oven for 10 minutes, turning halfway through, until lightly golden.

Combine the peanuts, sultanas and cheese in a bowl.

Carefully dip the toasted bread in the syrup until both sides are coated, then place enough bread slices in the baking dish to sit in a single layer. Spoon over a layer of the cheese mixture, then add another layer of toasted bread. Finish with the remaining cheese mixture and pour any left-over syrup over the top.

Transfer to the oven and bake for 30 minutes or until set.

Serve hot or cold.

PLATANOS FRITOS

The street-food vendors selling platanos fritos pipe out loud music to entice people out of their houses for an early-evening sugar bomb! This is when the platonas fritos cart rides through the streets looking for the best place to make a stop and calmly wait for the neighbourhood to line up.

I remember my sister Ana loving these and coming back home to top her fried plantains with even more jam! I've never been a huge fan of sweets, but now that I live on the other side of the world, I'd love to have a platanos fritos cart visit my neighbourhood now and again!

This recipe is for to all of you who, like my sister, have a sweet tooth.

SERVES 4

VEGETABLE OIL	250 ML (8½ FL OZ/1 CUP)
RIPE PLANTAINS, PEELED AND HALVED LENGTHWAYS	4
CONDENSED MILK	2 TABLESPOONS
STRAWBERRY JAM	80 G (2¾ OZ)
BROWN SUGAR	1 TABLESPOON
MARIE (RICH TEA) BISCUITS	8–12
CHOCOLATE OR RAINBOW SPRINKLES	TO SERVE
VANILLA ICE CREAM (OPTIONAL)	TO SERVE

Heat the oil in a large frying pan over medium–high heat. Add the plantain and cook, turning frequently, for 4–5 minutes, until light golden. Transfer to a plate lined with paper towel to drain.

Divide the plantain among four serving plates and top with the condensed milk, jam, sugar, biscuits and sprinkles. Serve with vanilla ice cream if you like.

PASTEL DE TRES LECHES

THREE MILK CAKE

This milky cake reminds me of all the 'quinceañera' parties I attended when I was a teenager. Fifteenth birthday parties are lavishly celebrated in Mexico and pastel de tres leches always makes an appearance. With vanilla whipped cream and delicious fresh fruit, it is the perfect celebration cake. Feel free to decorate it with your favourite toppings. Go wild!

SERVES 10

PLAIN (ALL-PURPOSE) FLOUR, PLUS EXTRA FOR DUSTING	185 G (6½ OZ/1¼ CUPS)
BAKING POWDER	1 TEASPOON
TABLE SALT	PINCH
FREE-RANGE EGGS	5
CASTER (SUPERFINE) SUGAR	230 G (8 OZ/1 CUP)
VANILLA ESSENCE	1 TEASPOON
UNSALTED BUTTER, MELTED THEN COOLED, PLUS EXTRA FOR GREASING	125 G (4½ OZ)
MILK TOPPING	
CONDENSED MILK	395 ML (13½ FL OZ)
EVAPORATED MILK	375 ML (12½ FL OZ)
BRANDY	30 ML (1 FL OZ)
REDUCED-FAT CREAM	250 ML (8½ FL OZ/1 CUP)
VANILLA ESSENCE	1 TEASPOON
TO DECORATE	
CANNED WHIPPED CREAM	200 G (7 OZ)
STRAWBERRIES, HULLED AND HALVED	200 G (7 OZ)
PEACHES IN SYRUP, DRAINED AND SLICED	50 G (1¾ OZ)

Preheat the oven to 180°C (350°F).

Grease a 23 cm (9 in) round cake tin and dust it with flour.

Combine the flour, baking powder and salt in a bowl. One by one add the eggs to the bowl, incorporating each egg before adding the next, then mix using electric beaters on low speed until combined. Increase the speed to medium and slowly add the sugar and vanilla, beating for 2 minutes or until you have a fluffy, yellow batter. Add the cold melted butter, then reduce the speed to low and beat for a further 5 minutes.

Spoon the batter into the prepared tin and use a spatula to spread it into an even layer. Gently tap the tin on your work surface to remove any air bubbles, then transfer to the oven and bake for 35 minutes or until the cake has a light golden crust and a skewer inserted into the middle of the cake comes out clean. Set aside to cool completely.

To make the milk topping, combine the ingredients in a bowl and stir until the mixture is smooth without any lumps.

Using a spatula, gently loosen the cake, then invert it onto a deep tray or serving plate. Use a fork to poke small holes all over the surface of the cake, then slowly pour over the milk topping, allowing the cake to absorb some of the topping before adding more.

Cover the cake with a thick layer of whipped cream and use a spatula to smooth the surface. Decorate the top with the strawberry and peach slices, then cut into slices and serve.

BAS

ICS

BASICS
BASICS
BASICS

Few Mexican dishes are complete without the addition of masa in one form or another. From tortillas and quesadillas to sopes, tlacoyos, huaraches and gorditas, masa forms the backbone of Mexican cuisine. Thankfully, it's very easy to make and it only takes a few minutes to combine flour, water and a little oil into a flexible dough, which can then be pressed into whatever shape your recipe calls for. A tortilla press will be your friend here, and although I recommend using a comal for cooking, a frying pan will do the job just as well.

This chapter also contains recipes for the salsas served with many of the dishes in this book. Here, chillies play a pivotal role and understanding how their flavours and heat profiles contribute to salsas will arm you with some serious Mexican culinary knowledge! If you have a favourite salsa, make a big batch and keep it in the fridge to serve with everything.

Finally, we look at how to prepare beans. Black beans and pinto beans are the most commonly used in Mexican cuisine, and understanding how to properly cook these simple ingredients will add authenticity to your chosen dish.

Cooked beans can be served as an accompaniment, but more frequently they are boiled, then mashed to make refried beans, which are then added to tacos and tortas, or even combined with masa dough to make an unctuous, rich dough which is then topped with fresh ingredients and, of course, salsa.

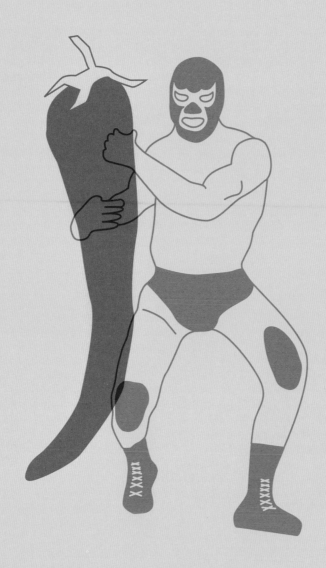

CORN AND TORTILLAS

Corn might seem like a mundane grain to some, but for Mexicans it is the cornerstone of our cuisine with a divine origin. Maize has been cultivated by Mesoamerican cultures for over 10,000 years, making it one of the world's oldest crops. Ancient cultures including the Olmecs, Aztecs and Mayans worshipped maize gods and associated the grain with life and fertility. It is still considered the 'golden grain', and remains a fundamental part of the Mexican diet.

From corn comes, of course, tortillas and the importance of this simple food in Mexican cuisine cannot be underestimated. Not only are they an accompaniment to nearly every meal, they are seen as a true reflection of Mexican identity.

Tortillas are made with yellow, white or blue masa flour and are then transformed into countless Mexican dishes. Below are a few of the most popular dishes eaten at restaurants, street food stalls and around family dinner tables all over Mexico.

TACOS = FILLED TORTILLAS	ENCHILADAS = TORTILLAS SOAKED IN SALSA	ENTOMATADAS = TORTILLAS SOAKED IN TOMATO SAUCE	CHILAQUILES = TOTOPOS SOAKED IN SALSA
QUESADILLAS = FOLDED TORTILLAS FILLED WITH CHEESE AND/OR PROTEIN AND GRILLED	ENCHILADAS SUIZA = ENCHILADAS WITH MELTED CHEESE	TOSTADAS = DEEP-FRIED TORTILLAS	SOUPS = DEEP-FRIED TORTILLA STRIPS
TACOS DORADOS OR FLAUTAS = FILLED AND DEEP-FRIED TORTILLAS	ENFRIJOLADAS = TORTILLAS SOAKED IN A BEAN SAUCE	TOTOPOS = DEEP-FRIED TORTILLA TRIANGLES	

BASICS

TORTILLAS

There is no doubt that handmade tortillas are far superior to store-bought versions, plus they are fun to make. They also enable you to use yellow, white or blue masa flour. Even though nixtamal (the process of soaking and cooking corn in limewater) is the traditional and most authentic way to make masa, it's very labour-intensive. Store-bought masa is absolutely fine to use and the results are pretty much the same. You will need a tortilla press to make tortillas. You can easily pick one up at your local Latin American supermarket or online.

MAKES ABOUT 20 CORN TORTILLAS

MASA FLOUR	500 G (1 LB 2 OZ)
WARM WATER	600 ML (20½ FL OZ)
TABLE SALT	PINCH
VEGETABLE OIL	50 ML (1¾ FL OZ)
VEGETABLE OIL SPRAY	FOR COOKING

Combine the masa, warm water, salt and oil in a bowl until you have a soft and non-sticky dough.

Lightly spray a comal or heavy-based frying pan with oil spray and place over medium–high heat.

Place a square of plastic wrap over the bottom half of a tortilla press. To make 16 cm (6¼ in) tortillas, roll 50 g (1¾ oz) of the dough into a ball and place it in the middle of the tortilla press. Cover with another square of plastic wrap (this stops the dough sticking to the press), then close the tortilla press and gently press to flatten the dough into a 3 mm (⅛ in) thick tortilla. If you are making 11 cm (4¼ in) tortillas, reduce the quantity of dough to 35 g (1¼ oz) for each tortilla.

Open the tortilla press, remove the top layer of plastic wrap and flip the tortilla onto your hand. Remove the bottom layer of plastic wrap and place the tortilla in the pan. Cook for about 2 minutes, then flip over and cook for another 2 minutes.

Transfer the tortilla to a tortilla warmer or folded tea towel and repeat with the remaining dough, using more oil spray as needed.

NOTES

Don't pre-roll the masa dough into balls, as they will dry up, causing the tortillas to crack.

If you are not eating the tortillas straight away, make sure you place them in a tortilla warmer. Keep in mind that handmade tortillas are meant to be eaten as you make them.

SOPES

Sopes are thick tortillas with a small rim to help contain their filling. In Mexico, food vendors make them to order. They can be large or small depending on whether you're after a snack or something more substantial. I personally like to make mine the same size as regular tortillas and eat them as a main meal.

MAKES ABOUT 10

VEGETABLE OIL SPRAY	FOR COOKING
TORTILLA DOUGH (SEE OPPOSITE)	1 x QUANTITY

Lightly spray a comal or heavy-based frying pan with oil spray and place over medium–high heat.

Place a square of plastic wrap over the bottom half of a tortilla press. Roll 100 g (3½ oz) of the dough into a ball and place it in the middle of the tortilla press. Cover with another square of plastic wrap (this stops the dough sticking to the tortilla press), then close the tortilla press and gently press to flatten the dough into a disc at least 1 cm (½ in) thick (don't press all the way, as sopes are thicker than tortillas).

Open the tortilla press, remove the top layer of plastic wrap and flip the sope onto your hand. Remove the bottom layer of plastic wrap and place the sope in the pan. Cook for about 3 minutes each side until firm.

Fill a small bowl with cold water.

Remove the sope from the pan and place it on a clean work surface. Dip your fingers into the water, then pinch the edge of the sope to form a rim.

Repeat with the remaining dough to make 10 sopes.

SOPES

ARROZ MEXICANO

 MEXICAN RICE

Mexican rice, also known as red rice, is a typical dish served in every home throughout Mexico. I remember coming home from school every day for lunch and the table would be laid out with warm tortillas, Mexican rice, beans and a good salsa!

SERVES 4

LONG-GRAIN RICE	250 G (9 OZ)
TOMATOES, ROUGHLY CHOPPED	3
WHITE ONION	½
TOMATO PASTE (CONCENTRATED PURÉE)	2 TABLESPOONS
TABLE SALT	30 G (1 OZ)
CHICKEN STOCK OR WATER	600 ML (20½ FL OZ)
VEGETABLE OIL	200 ML (7 FL OZ)
GARLIC HEADS, CLOVES PEELED	2
CARROTS, CUT INTO 3 CM (1¼ IN) DICE	2
FLAT-LEAF PARSLEY STALKS, CHOPPED	5
FRESH JALAPENO CHILLIES	2
WHITE OR YELLOW FRESH OR TINNED CORN KERNELS	100 G (3½ OZ)
FRESH OR FROZEN GREEN PEAS	50 G (1¾ OZ)
CORIANDER (CILANTRO) SPRIGS	TO SERVE
LEMON CHEEKS	TO SERVE

Soak the rice in a bowl of water for 10 minutes. Drain.

Place the tomato, onion, tomato paste, salt and chicken stock or water in a blender and blend until smooth.

Heat the oil in a large saucepan over medium–low heat. Add the garlic and cook, stirring, for 1–2 minutes until lightly browned. Using a slotted spoon, remove the garlic cloves and discard. Add the drained rice to the pan and stir for 4–5 minutes, until lightly toasted. Add the blended tomato mixture, carrot and parsley, then cover and cook for 5 minutes.

Score 5 mm (¼ in) long slits all over the jalapenos, then add them to the pan. Gently stir the rice, then cover and continue to cook, adding up to 250 ml (8½ fl oz/1 cup) more water if the mixture starts to look dry, for a further 10 minutes or until the liquid has evaporated and the rice is cooked through. Add the corn and green peas and stir through until warm.

Transfer the rice to serving bowls and serve with coriander sprigs and lemon cheeks.

FRIJOLES NEGROS

BLACK BEANS

Throughout my childhood, frijoles negros were a staple on the dinner table. I was quite a fussy eater back then, but I'd never refuse a bowl of warming black beans. Served with eggs or salsa, in a torta, taco, soup or refried, the possibilities are endless!

MAKES 1 KG (2 LB 3 OZ)

DRIED BLACK BEANS	300 G (10½ OZ)
DRIED BAY LEAF	1
DRIED OR FRESH EPAZOTE (OPTIONAL)	PINCH
WHITE ONION	½
TABLE SALT	15 G (½ OZ)

Rinse the beans and remove any grit or small rocks, then place in a large bowl and cover with water. Set aside to soak overnight.

Drain and rinse the beans, then place in a large saucepan with the remaining ingredients and 1.5 litres (51 fl oz/6 cups) water. Bring to the boil over high heat and boil for 30 minutes, then reduce the heat to medium and simmer for a further 40 minutes or until the beans are soft and cooked through. If the pan starts to dry out, add up to 250 ml (8½ fl oz/1 cup) more water. Remove and discard the bay leaf and onion, transfer the frijoles to a bowl and serve or add to your dish of choice.

The frijoles will keep in an airtight container in the fridge for up to 5 days.

BASICS

FRIJOLES CHARROS

This dish is most common in northern Mexico, but you can find it in Mexico City where it's served as side dish to tacos de bistec (steak tacos) and costillas (ribs). Some taquerias also serve it as a snack or appetiser, but it's quite rich so I like to serve it with tortillas and salsa verde as a more substantial meal.

SERVES 4

DRIED PINTO BEANS	500 G (1 LB 2 OZ)
DRIED BAY LEAF	1
DRIED OR FRESH EPAZOTE (OPTIONAL)	PINCH
WHITE ONION	1
TOMATOES, DICED	2
MINCED GARLIC	1 TEASPOON
CHIPOTLE CHILLI IN ADOBO SAUCE, CHOPPED	1
TABLE SALT	15 G (½ OZ)
VEGETABLE OIL OR PORK LARD	3 TABLESPOONS
FRESHLY GROUND BLACK PEPPER	PINCH
CHILLI POWDER	PINCH
DRIED OREGANO	PINCH
BACON SLICES, CUT LENGTHWAYS INTO 5 MM (¼ IN) THICK STRIPS	5
DICED BACON	50 G (1¾ OZ)
PORK SAUSAGES, CUT INTO 5 MM (¼ IN) DICE	3
COOKED MEXICAN-STYLE CHORIZO, CRUMBLED	30 G (1 OZ)
PORK CRACKLING (SEE PAGE 71), CRUMBLED	20 G (¾ OZ)
MEXICAN LAGER, PLUS EXTRA IF NEEDED	375 ML (12½ FL OZ)
LONG GREEN OR JALAPENO CHILLIES, DICED	4
CORIANDER (CILANTRO) LEAVES (OPTIONAL)	TO SERVE

Rinse the beans and remove any grit or small rocks, then place in a large bowl and cover with water. Set aside to soak overnight.

Drain and rinse the beans, then place in a large saucepan with the bay leaf and epazote (if using). Chop the onion in half and add a whole half to the pan. Cover with 2 litres (68 fl oz/8 cups) water, then bring to the boil over high heat and boil for 30 minutes. Reduce the heat to medium and simmer for a further 40 minutes or until the beans are soft and cooked through. If the pan starts to dry out, add up to 250 ml (8½ fl oz/1 cup) more water. Remove from the heat and set aside.

Roughly chop the remaining onion half, then place in a bowl with the tomato, garlic, chipotle chilli and salt and mix to combine.

Heat the oil or lard in a frying pan over medium–high heat. Add the tomato mixture and cook, stirring frequently, for 5 minutes. Add the black pepper, chilli powder and oregano and cook for a further 3 minutes.

Add the bacon, sausage, chorizo and crackling to the pan, along with the lager and stir to combine. Cook, stirring, for 20 minutes or until the beer has evaporated.

Transfer the sausage mixture to the beans and cook over medium heat for 20 minutes. If the frijoles charros start to dry out add a little water or more beer – the consistency should look like a thick soup.

Transfer to serving bowls, top with the chilli and coriander (if using) and serve.

Any left-over beans will keep in an airtight container in the fridge for up to 5 days.

BASICS

GUACAMOLE

When I was a child, I remember my dad loved to eat guacamole and chicharron rolled up in a taco. Now, of course, guacamole is everywhere, most commonly eaten as a dip with tortilla chips. It's actually extremely easy to make; it just depends on the avocados you use. In Mexico, we are lucky enough to have a huge variety of avocados at our disposal, but outside of the country there is less choice. I recommend using hass or fuerte avocados, as they are large, creamy and easy to peel.

MAKES 500 G (1 LB 2 OZ)

RIPE AVOCADOS (THE BIGGER THE BETTER)	5
TABLE SALT	15 G (½ OZ)
GREEN CHILLIES, SUCH AS JALAPENO, SERRANO OR CAYENNE, FINELY CHOPPED	3
CORIANDER (CILANTRO) LEAVES, FINELY CHOPPED	100 G (3½ OZ)
LIMES, JUICED	3
EXTRA VIRGIN OLIVE OIL	1 TABLESPOON

Gently mash the avocado in a bowl and stir through the remaining ingredients. Your guacamole is ready!

Guacamole is best eaten on the day it is made, as the avocado will start to discolour once peeled, but if you do have leftovers it will keep in an airtight container in the fridge for 1–2 days.

Boom!

NOTE	You can add two diced tomatoes if you like.

BASICS

PICO DE GALLO

FRESH SALSA

Pico de gallo reminds me of my dad's restaurant El Cuervo Cantina. I used to help him make this salsa, among others, and it's where I started my Mexican food journey. Pico de gallo is the perfect salsa to serve with tortilla chips. It also makes a great side salad.

MAKES ABOUT 320 G (11½ OZ)

WHITE ONION, DICED	½
GREEN JALAPENO OR SERRANO CHILLIES, FINELY CHOPPED	4
CORIANDER (CILANTRO) LEAVES, FINELY CHOPPED	200 G (7 OZ)
LIMES, JUICED	2
TABLE SALT	1 TEASPOON
FIRM TOMATOES, CUT INTO 3 CM (1¼ IN) CHUNKS	3

Place the onion, chilli and coriander in a bowl. Add the lime juice and salt and gently stir for 3 minutes. Add the tomato, stir to combine and serve.

Zap!

SALSA VERDE

GREEN SALSA

Salsas are one of the most important accompaniments in Mexican cuisine, and salsa verde is probably the most popular, with its the tangy flavour of green tomatillos mixed with fresh chilli. It's also my favourite salsa.

Fresh tomatillos are one of the ingredients Mexican expats miss most, but tinned tomatillos are readily available and are nearly as good. You will find them at Latin American supermarkets or online.

MAKES ABOUT 250 ML (8½ FL OZ/1 CUP)

FRESH OR TINNED TOMATILLOS	300 G (10½ OZ)
GREEN CHILLIES, SUCH AS JALAPENO, SERRANO OR LONG, ROUGHLY CHOPPED	10
WHITE ONION, ROUGHLY CHOPPED	½
GARLIC CLOVE, FINELY CHOPPED	½
TABLE SALT	1 TEASPOON
CORIANDER (CILANTRO) LEAVES, FINELY CHOPPED	100 G (3½ OZ)

If you are lucky enough to find fresh tomatillos, remove the husks and thoroughly wash the fruit. If using tinned tomatillos, drain and rinse them. Roughly chop the tomatillos.

Heat a comal or heavy-based frying pan over medium–high heat. Add the tomatillos, chillli and onion and cook, stirring frequently, until charred on all sides.

Place the charred tomatillos, onion and chilli in a mortar or blender and add the garlic, salt and 250 ml (8½ fl oz/1 cup) water. Pound with a pestle or blend the ingredients to a chunky salsa. Stir through the coriander and transfer to a serving bowl.

SALSA ROJA

RED SALSA

Salsa roja can be served fresh or cooked. I prefer the fresh version, but I recommend eating it on the day it's made, as the tomatoes are delicate and start to collapse into a liquidy mess after a few hours.

MAKES ABOUT 250 ML (8½ FL OZ/1 CUP)

LARGE TOMATOES, CHOPPED	4
WHITE ONION, ROUGHLY CHOPPED	½
DRIED CHILLIES DE ÁRBOL OR PEQUIN CHILLIES	3
GARLIC CLOVE, FINELY CHOPPED	½
TABLE SALT	1 TEASPOON
CORIANDER (CILANTRO) LEAVES, CHOPPED	50 G (1¾ OZ)
VEGETABLE OIL (IF MAKING COOKED SALSA)	3 TABLESPOONS

Heat a comal or heavy-based frying pan over high heat. Add the tomato and onion and cook, stirring frequently, for about 7 minutes until slightly charred.

Place the dried chillies in a small saucepan. Cover with 250 ml (8½ fl oz/1 cup) water and bring to the boil over high heat. Cook for 5–8 minutes, until the chillies are soft. Set aside to cool for 5 minutes, then remove any stalks.

Place the charred onion and tomato in a mortar or blender and add the garlic, chillies and their cooking water and the salt. Pound with a pestle or blend the ingredients to a chunky salsa. Stir through the coriander and transfer to a serving bowl.

To cook the salsa, heat the oil in a small saucepan over medium–high heat. Add the salsa and cook, stirring, for 7 minutes or until heated through and slightly reduced. The salsa is ready when the colour changes to a dark orange.

Set aside to cool before serving.

> **NOTE**
> Chillies de árbol and pequin chillies are very hot, but you can add more if you prefer an even spicier salsa.

SALSA TAQUERA

In Mexico City, food vendors make fresh salsa taquera at their stalls using a huge mortar and pestle. With its strong aroma of freshly pounded chillies, customers are enticed in to order tacos topped with this spicy, heavenly sauce. Every stall has their own recipe and Mexican people rate their favourite taco stand based on how good their salsa is.

MAKES ABOUT 250 ML (8½ FL OZ/1 CUP)

FRESH OR TINNED TOMATILLOS	300 G (10½ OZ)
WHITE ONION, HALVED	½
GARLIC CLOVES	2
TOMATO	1
VEGETABLE OIL	100 ML (3½ FL OZ)
DRIED GUAJILLO CHILLIES	2
DRIED CHILLIES DE ÁRBOL (ALTERNATIVELY USE FRESH CAYENNE OR THAI RED CHILLIES)	10
TABLE SALT	10 G (⅓ OZ)

If you are lucky enough to find fresh tomatillos, remove the husks and thoroughly wash the fruit.

Place half the onion, the garlic, tomato, tomatillos, 1 tablespoon of the oil and 500 ml (17 fl oz/2 cups) water in a saucepan. Bring to the boil over high heat and cook for 3 minutes. Remove from the heat, cover the pan and set aside to cool to room temperature.

Heat 2 tablespoons of the remaining oil in a frying pan over low heat. Add the guajillo chillies and cook, stirring, for 3 minutes on both sides, making sure the chillies don't burn. Using a slotted spoon, remove the chillies and add them to the ingredients in the saucepan. Repeat this step with the chillies de árbol.

Meanwhile, finely chop the remaining onion.

Transfer the contents of the pan to a large mortar or blender, add the salt and pound with a pestle or blend to a chunky salsa. Place the salsa in a serving bowl, stir through the finely chopped onion and serve.

Store the salsa in an airtight container in the fridge for up to 1 week.

BASICS

SALSA MACHA

 **BRAVE SALSA**

Salsa macha is one of my dad's signature salsas at my Mexican deli in Sydney. It packs a punch in the spice department, but it keeps you coming back for more! Because of the amount of heat in this salsa, Mexicans don't usually serve it in tacos; instead we use it as a spread in quesadillas and tortas. Add crushed peanuts for extra flavour.

MAKES ABOUT 300 ML (10½ FL OZ)

GARLIC CLOVES, THINLY SLICED	10
TABLE SALT	2 TEASPOONS
VEGETABLE OIL	100 ML (3½ FL OZ)
EXTRA VIRGIN OLIVE OIL, PLUS EXTRA IF NEEDED	200 ML (7 FL OZ)
DRIED CHILES DE ÁRBOL	25 G (¾ OZ)
DRIED PEQUIN CHILLIES	25 G (¾ OZ)
DRIED MORITA CHILLIES	10 G (⅓ OZ)

Combine the garlic and salt in a small bowl.

Heat the vegetable oil in a frying pan over medium heat. Add the salty garlic and cook, stirring, for 4–5 minutes until light golden. Do not let the garlic burn, or your salsa will be bitter. Transfer the garlic oil to a glass bowl.

Heat the olive oil in a frying pan over low heat, add the dried chillies and cook, stirring, for 3 minutes or until the chiles de árbol darken in colour. Remove from the heat, set aside to cool slightly, then add the chillies and oil to the garlic oil. Set the mixture aside to cool to room temperature.

Transfer the chilli mixture to a blender and blend until smooth. Add a little more olive oil if you prefer a runnier consistency.

Store the salsa in an airtight container in the pantry for up to 6 months.